Twelve
Lessons in Truth—Aum

By

JULIANA McKEE

taken from

THE AQUARIAN GOSPEL OF JESUS, THE CHRIST

with quotations from

THE CHRISTIAN BIBLE

and from

THE FLASHLIGHTS OF TRUTH

Published by

J. F. ROWNY PRESS

LOS ANGELES, CAL.

MCMXXXI

Kessinger Publishing's Rare Reprints
Thousands of Scarce and Hard-to-Find Books!

We kindly invite you to view our extensive catalog list at:
http://www.kessinger.net

"THE PRINCE OF PEACE"
BY BERTHA VALERIUS

DEDICATION

PREFACE

As publisher of THE AQUARIAN GOSPEL OF
JESUS THE CHRIST, of which my father, LEVI (Levi
H. Dowling) was the transcriber, I express my deep ap-
preciation to Juliana McKee, writer of the present volume,
that my father's work has been used as the basis of this
condensed story of the life of Jesus the Christ, which will
become one of the text books in CHURCH TRUTH
UNIVERSAL—AUM, of Los Angeles, California.

LEO W. DOWLING.

Los Angeles, California,
October 17, 1930.

FOREWORD

AT the beginning of a new age, or cycle of time, Jehovah God, the Deity of our solar system, sends forth a chosen son to show humanity lost in the world of illusion, the way, through Christ, back to the Father's House—AUM.

Jesus came as the chosen son of Jehovah, to be the pattern and to give the message in the Piscean Age to humanity. Not understanding the depth of his message, humanity has lived largely in the letter of the teaching.

Although still active in the outer, the old dispensation has closed. In this New Day, the spiritual age, humanity will receive and comprehend the spirit essence of the message of the Great Master, Jesus Christ.

This is the great day of redemption for mankind, and many who have long been on the path of Truth will, by the help of Jehovah, follow Jesus Christ into the full light of Aum.

The Masters in the White Brotherhood are assisting humanity. They are God-Conscious individuals who have reached the Father's House, and abide in freedom divine. Commissioned by the Father, they labor with the children of earth as they climb the mountain of Truth; on the summit of which shines the supernal light of Aum.

INTRODUCTION

THESE lessons in Truth—Aum, are written in the vibration and under the guidance of the God-Conscious Masters in the White Brotherhood; Who are redeemed from the carnal illusion. They are Masters in Love, Wisdom, and Compassion, and They labor unceasingly with humanity.

The Aquarian Gospel of Jesus, the Christ, transcribed by Levi, is used in the services of the Church School of Church Truth, Universal—Aum, in connection with the Christian Bible and the message of Truth Absolute, brought forth in the books by Elizabeth Delvine King.

The Aquarian Gospel of Jesus, the Christ, contains the drama of Christianity, as enacted nearly two thousand years ago in Palestine. The transcriber, Levi, after years of preparation, attained unto the spiritual consciousness which permitted him to enter the realm of Spirit Intelligence, the Akasha; and, from the records, he brought forth this work as commissioned by the Holy Breath. (Aquarian Gospel, page 10).

It is the story of the Prince of Peace, The Christ, who came as a babe in Bethlehem, and traveled every way of life that man must tread. He was despised, rejected, and abused; was spit upon; was crucified; was buried in a tomb; but he revived, and rose a conqueror over death.

A thousand times he said to men: "I came to show the possibilities of man; what I have done all men may do, and what I am all men shall be.".

This story of the Christ contains the true philosophy of life, of death, and of the resurrection of the dead. It shows the spiral journey of the soul until the man of earth and God are one forevermore. (Aquarian Gospel, page 11.)

CONTENTS

11

Aum, Thou Silent One
O'ershadowing all Thy manifests,
Aum, Eternal One
That knows the heart within each breast,
Aum, That guides, sustains, and blesses all,
Enfold within Thy glowing Light
Each child, who hears Thy call.

Lesson I.

IN THE DAWN OF THE PISCEAN AGE

TWO thousand years ago, in the dawn of the Piscean age, Augustus Cæsar reigned in Palestine. Herod Antipas ruled in Jerusalem.

At Nazareth, in the province of Galilee, a child was born to Joachim, a master of the Jewish law, and Anna, his wife, of the tribe of Judah.

The child was named Mary, and at the age of three, she was taken to Jerusalem by her parents to receive the blessings of the priests. Being a seer, the high priest foresaw that Mary would be the mother of a great prophet, and her life was consecrated to the Lord. She lived within the temple until she reached the age of womanhood, and Hillel, chief of the sanhedrim taught her the precepts of the Jews. Then Mary returned to Nazareth, and was betrothed to Joseph, son of Jacob. Joseph was a carpenter and a devout Essene.

One day the angel Gabriel appeared to Mary, in her home, saying: "Hail, Mary, Hail! Once blessed in the name of God; twice blessed in the name of Holy Breath; thrice blessed in the name of Christ: for you are worthy, and will bear a son who shall be called Immanuel. His name is Jesus, for he saves his people from their sins." (Aquarian Gospel, 2:15, 16.)

In St. Luke 1:30, 31, 38, we read: "And the angel said unto her: 'Fear not Mary: for thou hast found favor with God: And behold thou shalt conceive in thy womb, and bring forth a son, and shalt call his name Jesus.' And Mary said: Behold the handmaid of the Lord; be it unto me according to thy word.' And the angel departed from her."

13

In the temple at Jerusalem the holy priest, Zacharias, served. His wife Elizabeth lived in the Hebron hills.

Gabriel came to Zacharias as he burned the incense in the temple, and announced, that a holy child, whose name was John, would be born to Elizabeth and Zacharias; and John would harbinger and prepare the way for the coming savior, who, the prophets had foretold, would come and redeem the people.

Of John, the prophet wrote: "Behold, I send Elijah unto you again before the coming of the Lord; and he will level down the hills and fill the valleys up, and pave the way for him who shall redeem. He will be honored in the sight of God, and he will drink no wine, and from his birth he will be filled with Holy Breath."

"And Gabriel stood before Elizabeth, as she was in the silence, in her home, and told her the words that he had said to Zacharias in Jerusalem." (Aquarian Gospel 2:9, 11, 12.)

In the Christian Bible we read: "But the angel said unto him: Fear not, Zacharias, for thy prayer is heard, and thy wife Elizabeth shall bear a son, and thou shalt call him John. And many of the children of Israel shall he turn to the Lord their God." St. Luke 1:13, 16.)

When Gabriel appeared to Mary in Nazareth, she believed his words and she hastened to her cousin Elizabeth; they rejoiced together and Mary remained ninety days; then she returned to Nazareth.

Before the birth of Jesus, Mary desired to see Elizabeth once more, and she and Joseph began to journey toward her home. They stopped at Bethlehem. There was no room at the Inn; but outside the city wall, in a cave, they found a place to rest.

At midnight the child was born. Three masters robed in white came and stood before the child, and said: "All strength, all wisdom and all love be yours, Immanuel." The hills were filled with light and the voices of masters were heard to say: "All glory be to God on high; peace,

peace on earth, good will to men." (Aquarian Gospel 3:7, 13.) And a great star shone above Jerusalem.

Three wise men of Persia knew a master had been born. Guided by the star, they began to journey with precious gifts to honor him. Reaching Jerusalem, they inquired where they might find the new-born king.

Herod, the ruler of Jerusalem, heard of the wise men, and sent a messenger to bring them to his court. He called in council all the masters of the law to learn about the child, born to be king. These masters of the law said: "The prophets long ago foretold that one would come to rule the tribes of Israel; that this Messiah would be born in Bethlehem."

Herod sent the magians to Bethlehem, and bade them return and tell him of the child.

They found the babe with Mary in a shepherd's home; they bestowed their gifts, and honored him. They had read Herod's wicked heart, and told the parents of Jesus that they might flee with him to Egypt. Then they journeyed homeward, but went not through Jerusalem.

That night the parents fled with Jesus to Egyptland, and in ancient Zoan they abode with Elihu and Salome.

Herod was enraged that the Magians did not return to tell him of the child, born to be a king. He heard of John, the infant, who was born to go before and prepare the people for the coming king; and he sent his guards to Bethlehem to slay the infants Jesus and John and all children not two years of age.

This order of Herod reached Elizabeth, and she hurried with John to secret caves in the hills.

Fulfilling Herod's orders, the guards returned to him saying: "We know that we have slain the infant king; but John, his harbinger we could not find." (Aquarian Gospel 6:9.)

Then guards were sent to Zacharias in the temple at Jerusalem to learn the hiding place of John. Zacharias told the guards that he did not know the hiding place, and they returned to Herod. Later, other of Herod's guards returned to Zacharias; and, as he stood in prayer before the altar, one approached and slew him. Zacharias died before the sanctuary of the Lord.

Elizabeth and John were found, and taken to Elihu and Salome in Zoan, Egypt.

In this ancient sacred school, Mary and Elizabeth were to receive lessons that they were to teach their sons.

Herod died upon his throne.

Before Elihu began his lessons, he said to Mary and Elizabeth: "You may esteem yourselves thrice blest, for you are chosen mothers of long promised sons, who are ordained to lay in solid rock a sure foundation stone on which the temple of the perfect man shall rest—a temple that shall never be destroyed. And these, your sons, will be the first to tell the news, and preach the gospel of good will to men, and peace on earth. We call these sons, Revealers of the Light; but they must have the light before they can reveal the light. And you must teach your sons, and set their souls on fire with love and holy zeal, and make them conscious of their missions to the sons of men."

Then Elihu taught in the sacred groves, the lessons these mothers were to teach their sons.

First he taught that God and man were one: but man through carnal mind debased himself and turned away from God, but Holy Breath would make them one again. He taught that naught but love could be the savior of the world; and God so loved the world that he clothed his son in flesh, that the world might comprehend; and Jesus, son of Mary, came to manifest that love to man. He taught, that purity of life must first express to prepare the way for love; and that John, son of Elizabeth, was purity expressed. He taught the unity of life; that every living thing was bound by cords to every other living thing; and that in man there was the higher and the lower self. The higher self, the Atman, was God expressed in man; the lower self, the carnal man, was an illusion and would pass away. That in the higher self, the real, were all the attributes of God; the lower self was but the reflex of the truth.

Elihu told these mothers to study well themselves, to know themselves. He said: "He who knows his lower self, knows the illusions of the world, knows of the things that pass away; and he who knows his higher self, knows God; knows well the things that can not pass away."

He taught, that evil was a myth; that it was part of the carnal dream in which man was enmeshed; and that it must pass away; that the only devil from which men must be redeemed is that of self, the lower self.

Later in Jesus' ministry he said: "I came to rescue man from himself."

Then Salome taught of God, the One, the Three, the Seven; that before the worlds were formed was God, the One, the Spirit, Universal Breath. In the teaching of the Absolute, the One Eternal God, the Universal Breath is Aum; the impersonal God unmanifest. Of God, the Three, Salome taught. When Spirit, God the One breathed forth the Father-God and Mother-God came forth; and when these two in union breathed their only Son, Love, the Christ was born; and when the Triune God breathed forth, lo! seven Spirits stood before the throne. These are the Elohim, Creative Spirits of the universe; and these made man in their own image.

In Genesis 1:27 we read: "So God created man in His own image, in the image of God created He him; male and female created He them."

In Truth Absolute we learn that Atman was created a perfect being by the God of Love and Wisdom, and that the full expression of this divine manifestation will come forth into outer expression when the carnal mind and heart of man have been purified. For Aum, and His Divine Creation within Himself is all there eternally is; all else will pass away.

In closing, Salome said: "Blessed is the man whose spirit is triumphant and whose lower self is purified; whose soul is cleansed."

Elihu taught that in ancient times, in the east, people worshiped God, the One, whom they called Brahm. They lived in wisdom's way and were in peace until selfishness arose among the priests. They changed the laws from justice to suit the carnal mind. In the darkness of that age some great masters stood, they were the beacon lights before the world; and they preserved the wisdom of their holy Brahm in sacred books.

In Chaldea, a pious Brahm lived whose name was Terah. His son called A-Bram was devoted to the Brahmic faith, and he was set apart to be the father of the Hebrew race. Abram journeyed to the land of Canaan, and when the famine came he journeyed with his kin to Egypt and lived in Zoan. There he learned the wisdom of the wise. Then he took his flocks and kin again to Canaan where he died. His life and works are preserved in the Jewish Sacred books.

Elihu also taught that in Persia religion grew corrupt. The people worshiped many Gods; but Truth was brought to light when Zarathustra came. From Persia came the Magians who were the first to greet Mary's son as the Prince of Peace. The Avesta contains the precepts and laws of Zarathustra. Elihu taught that words were naught until they became alive and were a part of head and heart. That Truth is one; but no one knows the truth until he is the truth.

He taught that darkness and corruption expressed in India until the great Lord Buddha came and brought the light. That Buddha's creed was justice, love, and righteousness, and that he preached the gospel of a higher life. The words of Buddha are recorded in the Indian sacred books and they are part of the instructions of the Holy Breath.

Elihu said: "The land of Egypt is the land of secret things. The mysteries of the ages lie lock-bound in our temples and our shrines. The masters of all times and climes come here to learn; and when your sons have grown to manhood they will finish all their studies in Egyptian schools."

Next morning when the sun arose the masters and their

pupils were in the sacred grove, and here Salome taught
that the fount of prayer was in the heart, and there they
prayed in silence, and every heart was blest. Then Elihu
told Mary and Elizabeth they need not tarry longer there;
that their lessons were all completed. He said: " A mighty
work is given you to do; you shall direct the minds that
will direct the world. Your sons are set apart to lead men
up to righteous thoughts, and words, and deeds; to make
men know the sinfulness of sin; to lead them from the
adoration of the lower self and all illusive things; and
make them conscious of the self that lives with Christ in
God."

He told them of the trials and temptations which their
sons would meet; that they would go to many countries,
and sit at the feet of many masters to learn like other
men.

After three years with Elihu and Salome; Mary, Joseph,
and Elizabeth, with Jesus and his harbinger, John, set
forth upon their homeward way. They journeyed by the
Bitter Sea, and at the home of Joshua they rested. Elizabeth and John remained with this near of kin; but Joseph,
Mary, and Jesus returned to their home in Nazareth.

The childhood of John, the harbinger, was spent in the
Engedi hills, over which he used to roam, for he loved the
wilderness. Elizabeth taught him the lessons of Elihu and
Salome, and he delighted in them. When they were completed John went to live in David's cave with Matheno,
a priest of Egypt from the temple of Sakara. Matheno
taught him day by day, and opened up to him the mysteries of life.

John loved his master, who was an Israelite; and when
the Jewish feast-time came, Matheno took him to Jerusalem. He was nine years old, and was delighted with this
visit. Matheno told him about the services of the Jews,
the meaning of the sacrifices and rites. John could not
understand how sin could be blotted out by sacrifice of
bird and animal. Matheno told him this sacrifice was borrowed from idol worshipers of other lands, who believed

it blotted out their sins; but he taught John that sin was never blotted out through sacrifice of bird or animal; that sin was the rushing forth of man into the fens of wickedness, and to blot out sin one must retrace his steps and purify his heart by love and righteousness. Thus sin was forgiven, for forgiveness was the paying up of debts.

Matheno taught John of the sacred books of olden times; that the spirits of the Holy One cause things to come and go in proper time. That universal law expressed in seed and harvest time; and, as in nature, so in the needs of man, this law expressed, and as man had need for greater light, a holy One appeared to give the light, and that the sacred books of all ages in their proper time were for man's enlightenment. He taught John that man had within himself free will, the power to choose; that he might reach the greatest heights or sink unto the lowest depths; that the battle ground was in himself; and that he must conquer carnal self to rise unto the heights; that the Holy Ones just light the way.

Matheno said: "Men have need for greater light; now the Day Star from on high begins to shine; and Jesus is the flesh made messenger to show that light to men. And you, my pupil, you have been ordained to harbinger the coming day."

Thus John was taught to lead the way for man through purity of heart to see the light.

Matheno said: "In the ages yet to come, man will attain to greater heights, and lights still more intense will come. And then, at last, a mighty master soul will come to earth to light the way up to the throne of perfect man."

John was twelve years old when his mother passed, and he was deeply grieved. Matheno comforted the child, and said: "It is not well to weep because of death; your mother's tasks are finished; it is but selfishness that makes one wish to call again to earth departed souls. Then let your mother rest in peace. Just let her noble life be strength and inspiration unto you."

Matheno said: "You are to lead a life of purity, and teach men to cleanse and purify their lives." He took John to the Jordan ford and he was washed, symbolic of the cleansing of the soul by purity of life; and he gave John the inner meaning of this rite, that he might wash the multitudes.

They went then to the temple of Sakara in Egypt in the valley of the Nile. John was received with joy, and was called the Brother Nazarite. John lived for eighteen years within this temple. He conquered self and learned the duties of the harbinger.

Now in her home in Nazareth, on Marmion Way, Mary gave to Jesus the lessons of Elihu and Salome. Jesus loved the Vedic Hymns, the Avesta, the Psalms of David, and the words of Solomon. At seven years of age he knew the Jewish books of prophecy by memory.

Joachim said to Jesus on his seventh birthday, that he would give him, in remembrance of the day, whatever he desired. Jesus said that he was satisfied, but he desired that he give a feast that he might bring the needy ones to share with them. Joachim said: "Tis well" and Jesus ran to every needy child and soon three-score of them followed him up Marmion Way. Jesus and his mother served the feast, and all were glad.

One day Rabbi Barachi of the synagogue in Nazareth asked Jesus which of the ten commands was greatest. Jesus said he did not see a greatest of the commands, he saw them all as one; that love bound the ten together in one bond; and added: "If one is full of love he can do nothing else than worship God; for God is Love, and if one is full of love he does not need commands of any kind."

During the feast time in Jerusalem Jesus watched the butchers kill the lambs and birds for sacrifice, and his heart was touched. He said to the priest: "Why do you burn their flesh before the Lord?" The priest replied: "This is our sacrifice for sin." And Jesus said: "Did not David say that God requires not a sacrifice for sin? Did not

Isaiah say the same?" He then sought out Hillel, chief of the Sanhedrim, and asked if he could not help him find the God of Love, that his God was not one of cruelty.

Jesus remained in Jerusalem with Hillel a year and learned many lessons and the Jewish precepts, and Jesus gave Hillel many lessons on the higher life. He then returned to Nazareth.

At twelve, again Jesus visited Jerusalem with his parents. He went within the temple, and disputed with the masters of the law. He read from the book of prophecy. Hillel asked him if he would interpret that which he had read, and Jesus said: "One law abides; it is justice, and God is just. He who breaks this law must suffer; for, as man sows, so must he also reap. Israel must return to ways of holiness, or other nations will come and sack Jerusalem, and tear the temple down, and take the people captive to foreign lands. That the people would wander as sheep without a shepherd; but in time God would bring them back again. That after many years the temple would be built again; and one would come to glorify the house of God."

While on their homeward journey, Jesus' parents missed him. They returned to Jerusalem and found him in the temple, and to his mother's questioning he answered: "I must be about my Father's work." He bade the masters of the law farewell, and returned to Nazareth, and worked with Joseph as carpenter. To him the tools he used were all symbolic of the tools that man must use to purify his mind, and bring his temple to perfection. (Aquarian Gospel Chapters 1-20 in part).

When man, in his search for Truth, learns his own limitations, he desires assistance from above. He then asks, seeks, and knocks; and the door is opened. He is assisted from the carnal dream and its illusions into the light of Truth, and perceives God's great plan for humanity. Moving onward in the footsteps of the Masters, he gradually comes into the realization of himself as God's divine child, Atman, and of God's spiritual creation, in which Atman abides.

It is the destiny of every soul to attain unto perfection. This requires the Father's help, and the assistance of the Great Ones who have attained. No one in the carnal dream can pass into the reality alone; for the reality is in another dimension.

Jesus was the love of God made manifest. He came as a pattern for the human race, that each soul might attain unto perfection. Following in his path, led by the God-Conscious Redeemed Ones, humanity, one by one, wind their way back to the Reality, the Father's House— AUM.

When man reaches perfection, he expresses the Atman Self, God's Love made manifest in perfect form, the real Self which has never been contaminated in Its journey through experience. Atman then knows himself to be the Son of God, and the Crowning Glory of His Creation.

LESSON II.

LIFE OF JESUS IN INDIA

IN our Christian bible, we have no record of Jesus' life from the time he left the temple at Jerusalem with his parents, where he astonished the learned masters of the law with his understanding of spiritual life, and his question to his mother: "How is it that ye sought me? know ye not that I must be about my Father's business?" (St. Luke 2:49) until he was thirty years of age, when he began his Christine ministry.

In the Aquarian Gospel of Jesus, the Christ, we are given the story of his life and works, as he journeyed through other lands, during the intervening eighteen years.

In Jerusalem, while Jesus read and interpreted from the book of prophecy in the temple, he was heard by Ravanna, a royal prince of India. The prince was amazed to hear the words of Jesus, and sought him in Nazareth. Ravanna found the boy, and for certain days he was a guest at Jesus' home. He sought to learn his wisdom; but it was too great for him. He asked the parents if he might take their son to India, that Jesus might learn the teaching of the Brahms. The parents gave consent, and Jesus journeyed with Ravanna to his palace at Orissa.

The Brahmic priests welcomed home the prince, and Jesus was accepted with favor as a pupil in the temple Jagannath. Often he amazed the priests of the temple with his wisdom.

Lamaas, one of the priests, loved Jesus, and as they walked together he asked of him: "What is Truth?" Jesus said: "Truth is the only thing that changes not." And he told him of that which was the eternal reality, and of its opposite, the carnal dream. And to Lamaas' question: "What is man?" Jesus said: "Man is manifest of Truth. The carnal man does not comprehend it: but when he is quickened and awakened he learns the truth." And to the question: "What is understanding, wisdom, and faith, and salvation?" Jesus answered: "Understanding is the rock on which man builds himself: it is knowledge of the lower self. And wisdom is the consciousness that God and man are one. Faith is the surety of the omnipotence of God and man; the certainty that man will reach deific life. Salvation is a ladder reaching from the heart of man to the heart of God. It has three steps; Belief is first, and this is what man thinks, perhaps, is truth. And faith is next, and this is what man knows is truth. Fruition is the last, and this is man himself, the truth. Belief is lost in faith; and in fruition faith is lost; and man is saved when he has reached deific life, when he and God are one.

Jesus abode four years in the temple Jagannath. One day he asked to know the Brahmic views of castes. When he was told that the Holy One, Brahm, made men to suit himself and that all were not equal in his sight, he said: "Then Parabrahm is not a God of justice and of right, for with his own strong hand he has exalted one and brought another low." And looking upward he prayed to his Father-God, who held within his hands the scales of justice and right; who made all men equal, and said: "Thou Father of the human race, I praise thy name."

His prayer angered the priests, and they drove him from the temple. Jesus found shelter with the black and yellow men, the servants and tillers of the soil, and he taught them the gospel of equality, the brotherhood of man, the Fatherhood of God; and the universal prayer.

Jesus taught the common people in all the cities of Orissa of the possibilities of man; that each was a child of God and should be free. He told them to live the life of brotherhood, to cast away their idols, to make their hearts their altars, to burn their sacrifices with the fire of love, and to lay their gifts upon the tables of the poor.

He went then to the sacred city of Benares and there he taught the people of the One God; to whom each people give a different name. That the One God was omnipresent and was the causeless cause, the Rootless Root, from which all things have grown.

Ajainin, a Brahmic priest from Lahore came to Benares to learn of Jesus. The law forbade him to go among the Sudras where Jesus lived, and he sent a message inviting Jesus as a guest to dine with the priests at the temple. Jesus sent this word to Ajainin, The Holy One regards all men alike; the dwelling of my host is good enough for any council of the sons of men. If pride of caste keeps you away, you are not worthy of the light. My Father-God does not regard the laws of men.

Ajainin then came by night to learn about the ancient wisdom and about the kingdom of the Holy One. Jesus taught him that the kingdom is within the heart; that the king is universal love, the Christ; and he who entered through the gate of the kingdom must fall upon his knees, for it was low, that he could take no carnal bundles through. That the lower self must be transmuted to spirit self.

Ajainin said: "Can I become a subject of this King?" And Jesus said: "You are yourself a king, and you may enter through the gate and be a subject of the King of kings. But you must lay your priestly robes aside; must cease to serve the Holy One for gold; must give your life, and all you have, in willing sacrifice to the sons of men." The seeds of faith and brotherhood were sown in Ajainin's soul. As he journeyed to his home he seemed to sleep, to pass through darkest night, and when he awoke the Sun of Righteousness had arisen; he had found the king.

While in Benares Jesus received word of his father's death, and that his mother was deeply grieved, and that she longed to see him. He bowed his head in silent thought, then wrote these words of cheer: "My mother, all is well, is well with father, and is well with you. His work in this earth-round is done, and it is nobly done. Our Father-God is with him there, as he was with him here; and there his angel guards his footsteps lest he go astray. When grief comes trooping through the heart, just loose yourself; plunge deep into the ministry of love, and grief is not. Yours is a ministry of love, and all the world is calling out for love. Then let the past go with the past; rise from the cares of carnal things, and give your life for those who live; and, if you lose your life in serving, you will be sure to find it in the morning sun, the evening dews, in song of bird, in flowers, and in the stars of night. Strive then, to be content, and I will come to you some day, and bring you richer gifts than gold or precious stones. I am sure that John will care for you, supplying all your needs; and I am with you all the way, Jehoshua." He sent the letter on its way to Jerusalem.

Jesus remained and taught in Benares many days. He shook the very foundation of the Brahmic teaching. The common people followed him, and this enraged the priesthood. Much confusion reigned, and the priests planned to rid their city of the Hebrew Sage.

Lamaas, hearing of the plan to take the life of Jesus, sent messengers to him, and he departed from the city. He journeyed to the north and reached the Himalayan mountains. He was welcome in the Buddhist temple in the city of Kapavistu.

With Barata Arabo, a Buddhist priest, Jesus read the sacred manuscripts. He rejected the Buddhist doctrine of the evolution of lower forms of life to higher forms and man, as mind, evolving through these forms.

Knowing the truth concerning God and his spiritual creation, he said: "Time never was when man was not. That which begins will have an end. If man was not, the time will come when he will not exist. From God's own Record Book we read: The Triune God breathed forth, and seven Spirits stood before his face. (The Hebrews call these seven Spirits, Elohim.) And these are they who, in their boundless power, created everything that is, or was. These Spirits of the Triune God moved on the face of boundless space, and seven ethers were; and every ether had its form of life. These forms of life were clothed in the substance of their ether planes. And with the eyes of soul all creatures see these ether planes and all the forms of life."

Barata was amazed, the wisdom of the Hebrew Sage was revelation unto him. Vidiyapati, wisest of the Indian sages, heard Jesus speak to Barata and to the priests of Kapavistu, he said: "This Hebrew prophet is the rising star of wisdom, deified. He brings to us a knowledge of the secret things of God; and all the world will hear his words, will heed his words, and glorify his name. You priests of Kapavistu, stay! be still and listen when he speaks; he is the living oracle of God." And all the priests gave thanks.

(Man is eternal, and that which is called the fall of man is but the wandering out of man from the divine consciousness within himself, into the outer and lower state, the illusion—the world. In the divine consciousness, Atman vibrates in the fourth dimension. In truth, Atman has never been separated from his source; he turned away from God; and in looking outward a mist arose, the mist of the carnal mind. When this mist is overcome, Atman will again be one with God.)

Jesus taught the common people of Kapavistu how to attain unto the joy of life. He told these unhappy toilers of the heaven within the heart. And then he journeyed on to Lassa, in Tibet. There in Lassa is a master's temple, rich in manuscripts of ancient lore; and there Meng-ste, greatest of the Eastern sages, welcomed Jesus. They read the sacred manuscripts, and often discussed the service best adapted for the coming age. Jesus did not teach in Lassa; when his studies were completed in the temple schools, he journeyed toward the West.

In a monastery in the city, Leh, he was received. There

he sought out the common people and taught and healed the sick. When he left he blessed them in silent benediction, and went his way to give the light to others.

In the Kashmar valley Jesus received a camel from a band of merchantmen, who had heard him speak and seen his mighty works in Leh. And he continued with them to Lahore.

Ajainin and some Brahmic priests received Jesus at Lahore. He taught them the healing art and many other things. He taught the common people, healed their sick, and showed them how to rise to better things by helpfulness.

While sitting with Ajainin on the temple porch one day, a band of wandering singers paused to sing and play. Jesus said: "Among the high bred people of the land we hear no sweeter music than these uncouth children of the wilderness bring to us. In one short life they could not gain such grace of voice, such knowledge of harmony and tone. Men call them prodigies. There are no prodigies. These people are not young. A thousand years would not suffice to give them such divine expressiveness, and such purity of voice and touch. Ten thousand years ago these people mastered harmony. And they have come again to learn still other lessons."

He could not tarry longer at Lahore. He bade the priests farewell, and journeyed on his camel to the Sind. (Aquarian Gospel, Chapters 21-37 in part.)

Jesus was led through India by Jehovah. He respected all the teachings that he heard, and as Jehovah flashed the truth to him, Jesus gave it forth.

Service was the keynote of his teaching, he said: "If you would live the perfect life, give forth your life in service for your kind, and for the forms of life that men esteem the lower forms of life."

Through serving God and all the manifests of His creation, a feeling of kinship with every living thing comes to man, and with it the realization that that which binds together all creation is the bond of Universal Love.

Love is the impersonal son of God, the Christ. Jesus, the Christ, became pure Love. He expressed this love to all humanity; that all souls might see the light of Truth and follow in its path.

In St. John, 8:12, Jesus said: "I am the light of the world: he that followeth me shall not walk in darkness, but shall have the light of life."

The light of life is Aum—the Absolute; and, to reach the Absolute, man must follow Jesus Christ, the Light and Lord of this planet. Following in His path each soul in time will bring forth into outer expression the Love which is Christ, the only begotten Son of God.

LESSON III.

LIFE OF JESUS IN PERSIA, ASSYRIA, AND GREECE

JOURNEYING homeward from India, Jesus came to the land of Persia. He reached Persepolis, the home of the three wise men, Hor, Lun, and Mer, who had seen his star rise above Jerusalem twenty-four years before, and had journeyed with costly gifts to honor the master of the age.

Feeling that Jesus was nearing Persepolis, these masters started forth to meet him; and, as they met, a great light shone about them. They reached the magi's home where Kaspar, Zara, and Melzone, wise men from the North, had come. They all rejoiced, and sat in silence seven days communing with the silent brotherhood.

In Persepolis, Jesus spoke to many people, who had gathered at a feast in honor of their magian God. Standing in their midst he said: "My brothers, sisters, children of our Father-God: Most blessed are you among the sons of men today, because you have such just conceptions of the Holy One and man. Your purity in worship and in life is pleasing unto God; and to your master, Zarathustra, praise is due." He said: "But in your sacred books we read that two among the seven creative spirits are of superior strength; that one of these created all the good; the other one created all that evil is." Jesus asked the masters how evil could be born of that which is all good? One arose and said: "If God, the one, made not this evil, then, where is the God who did?"

Jesus then explained the origin of evil. He said: "Whatever God, the One, has made is good, and like the first great Cause, the seven Spirits all are good, and every-

31

thing that comes from their creative hands is good. Now,
all created things have colors, tones, and forms their own;
but certain tones, though good and pure themselves, when
mixed, produce inharmonies, discordant tones. So evil is
the inharmonious blending of the colors, tones, and forms
of good. Now, man is not all-wise, and yet has will his
own. He has the power, and uses it, to mix God's good
things in a multitude of ways. And every tone and form,
be it good or ill, becomes a living thing. Man makes his
devil; and none can dissipate the evil one, but man who
made it thus." (Good and evil, the pairs of opposites,
exist only in the world of relativity, they are the product
of the carnal mind, and only in the carnal man's concept
do they exist. When the carnal man awakens from this
illusion, he perceives the light of Truth. In the divine
reality—Aum, the kingdom, all is Harmony, Love, and
Peace; this is Atman's home. Atman is the image and
likeness of God; His perfect creation in form, and in the
perfect creation He abides.)

In Flashlights of Truth, page 107, we read: "God's
Perfect Creation is sublime; and Love, Peace, and Harmony abide there. Not even one discordant note of Carnality can penetrate it; yet it is around and about man,
within him, and everywhere, and is never interfered with
in any way whatsoever by carnality and its expressions.
Seemingly, they intermingle; yet they do not, because a
shadow can not mingle with sunshine, though it expresses
in it; but should the sun disappear, there would be no
shadow. In other words, if there were not the Real, there
could be no counterfeit. God's perfect creation is God
made manifest, or the idea of God expressed."

When Jesus came again to teach the people of Persepolis, a great light shone about him. A Magus did not
comprehend this light and privately asked its meaning.
Jesus told him of the holy silence where the soul meets
God; and that those who enter there become immersed in
light. He said: "The silence is the kingdom of the soul
not seen by human eyes. None but the pure in heart may

enter there; the human will must be absorbed by the divine to come into a consciousness of holiness." He said: "Within the Holy Place, you will see upon the shrine the candle of the Lord aflame. And when you see it burning there, look deep within the temple of your brain, and you will see it all aglow. In every part, from head to foot, are candles all in place, just waiting to be lighted by the flaming torch of Love; and when you see the candles all aflame, just look, and you will see, with eyes of soul, the waters of the fount of wisdom rushing on; and you may drink, and there abide. And then the curtains part and you are in the Holiest of All, where rests the Ark of God, whose covering is the Mercy Seat. Fear not to lift the Sacred board; the Tables of the Law are in the Ark concealed. Take them and read them well; for they contain all precepts and commands that men will ever need. And then behold the manna there, the hidden bread of life; and he who eats shall never die. The Cherubim have guarded well for every soul this treasure box, and whosoever will may enter and find his own."

Jesus then went to the sacred groves of Cyrus to teach the multitudes and heal the sick. Many were near a healing fount waiting for the waters to become potentized by the Holy One. Jesus told them, that faith was the healing power of every drop of the water of the spring, and that he who believed could be made whole by washing in the fount. He said, that love and living faith would cleanse and free from sin. Many plunged into the fount in faith, and they were healed.

(In his teaching and healing Jesus spoke much of faith; without which, it is impossible to please God. "According to your faith be it unto you," he said to those who came for healing. A conscious living faith is vital for one who is endeavoring to attain the spirit life. It can not be manufactured by the mind of man. It is a gift from God. St. Paul tells us: "It is the evidence of things not seen.")

Jesus finished his work in Persia, and Kaspar journeyed

with him to the Euphrates. They pledged to meet again
in Egypt, and said farewell.

Jesus journeyed on to Chaldea. At Ur, where Abraham was born he tarried and taught. He told the people
their land was no more the fruitful land that Abraham
loved so well; but that soon the shepherds would be glad,
the deserts would rejoice, and the flowers bloom. He
preached the gospel of good will and peace on earth, and
told them of the brotherhood of life, and of the kingdom
of the soul.

Among the people stood Ashbina, greatest sage of
Assyria. He told the people to take heed of Jesus' words,
that he was the prophet of the living God.

Jesus and Ashbina went through many towns and cities
of Chaldea and the lands between the Tigris and the
Euphrates, and Jesus healed a multitude of people. They
went to Babylon not far away and there beheld the ruined
city where Israel's children were held in bondage after the
destruction of the holy city.

In the plains of Shinar, Jesus and Ashbina tarried seven
days in prayer regarding the needs of men, and how the
sages could best serve the coming age. Then Jesus
journeyed to his home in Nazareth. His mother rejoiced
to see him, and made a feast, and invited all their kin.
Jesus' brothers were not pleased; they laughed his claims
to scorn. Jesus told his mother and her sister, Miriam,
of his journeys, of his learning, and of his works in other
lands.

Jesus desired to study with the Grecian masters. He
left his home in Nazareth, and crossed the Carmel hills;
took ship at the port, and was soon in the Grecian Capitol.
He met Apollo and other Grecian masters who welcomed
him, and all the doors of Grecian learning were opened up
to him.

Jesus heard the wisest masters speak in the Areopagus;
but the wisdom he brought to them was far greater, and
he remained in Athens, and taught. He spoke in the
Amphitheater at Apollo's bidding, and he said: "Of all

the earth, there is no place more sensitized, more truly spirit-blest, than that where Athens stands. No other land has been the home-land of such mighty men of thought as grace your scrolls of fame. A host of sturdy giants of philosophy, of poetry, of science, and of art, were born upon the soil of Greece, and rocked to manhood in your cradle of pure thought; but all your high accomplishments are but stepping stones to worlds beyond the realm of sense; are but illusive shadows flitting on the walls of time. In science and philosophy there is no power strong enough to fit a soul to recognize itself, or to commune with God. Unaided by the Spirit-Breath, the work of intellection tends to solve the problems of the things we see, and nothing more. The senses were ordained to bring into the mind mere pictures of the things that pass away; they do not deal with real things; they do not comprehend eternal law."

He told them that man had within himself something that would tear the veil apart that he might see the world of real things. That it was Spirit Consciousness, and it became awakened when Holy Breath was a welcome guest.

He said: "There is no power in intellect to turn the key; philosophy and science both have toiled to get a glimpse behind the veil; but they have failed. The secret spring that throws ajar the door is touched by nothing else than purity in life, by prayer and holy breath." He urged them to mingle their clear waters of Grecian thought with the flood of Spirit life. The Grecian masters were astonished at the wisdom of Jesus' words.

Jesus taught the Grecian masters many days. They were delighted with his words; and though they could not fully comprehend, they accepted his teaching.

One day Apollo said to Jesus: Sir, if you would see the Delphic Oracle and hear it speak, you may accompany me. And Jesus and Apollo went in haste. When Apollo stood before the Oracle it spoke and said: "Apollo, sage of Greece, the bell strikes twelve; the midnight of the ages now has come. Within the womb of nature, ages are

conceived; they gestate, and are born in glory with the
rising sun, and when the agic sun goes down the age dis-
integrates and dies. The Delphic Age has been an age of
glory and renown: the gods have spoken to the sons of
men through oracles of wood, and gold, and precious
stone. The Delphic sun has set: the Oracle will go into
decline: the time is near when men will hear its voice no
more. The gods will speak to man by man. The Living
Oracle now stands within these sacred groves; the Logos
from on high has come. From henceforth will decrease my
wisdom and my power: from henceforth will increase the
wisdom and the power of him, Immanuel. Let all the
masters stay: let every creature hear and honor him. Immanuel."

(The Grecian masters attained great heights in the re-
lative world. Their teaching was the highest teaching that
can be given the intellect of man. But Jesus brought them
the wisdom of the Absolute.)

One day as Jesus walked upon the Athens beach, a
storm at sea arose. The people prayed frantically at their
shrines, regardless of the lives that were being lost. Jesus
rescued many: and, when the storm had ceased, he told
the people of the fruitlessness of praying to their idols to
stay the storm. He said: "The god that saves dwells in
your own souls and manifests in helping those in need.
And what you do for other men the Holy One will do
for you. And thus God helps."

His work in Greece was finished, and Jesus prepared to
leave. He commended the Grecian masters for their learning and royal hospitality, and told them of a time when
Greece would be a spirit power upon the earth: the time
when God would be their buckler and their strength. He
said farewell. The people wept. Apollo raised his hand
in silent benediction. (Aquarian Gospel, Chapters 38-46
in part.)

*   *   *   *

Throughout his journeys East and West Jesus healed

the sick, and brought a light that lifted the people from the darkness of idolatry of many gods, to the light of the One Eternal God, and of man's relationship to Him.

Aum, the One God, the Absolute, is the Truth of all ages. Through revelation this Truth is now coming to the humanity of this planet from the Divine Source, through the Divine Masters, Jesus Christ the head.

Love, the great Redeemer, leads man out from the shadowland into the Reality, into that "Light which lighteth every man that cometh into the world," the Atman Self. In the light of the Reality, he perceives the unity of life, the one God clothed in many manifested forms; the One Breath of God breathing through every living thing; the One Love Essence, which is the substance of all form; the One Power embracing and sustaining all within Itself, the One overshadowing, abiding Presence—Aum the Absolute and Atman—Man Divine.

LESSON IV.

LIFE OF JESUS IN EGYPT
PART ONE

JESUS journeyed to Egypt to seek admission to the temple of the Sacred Brotherhood. He tarried at Zoan many days with the aged teachers, Elihu and Salome, who had taught his mother twenty-five years before; when he was but a babe. He told them of his journeys and his works in other lands; of meeting the masters of these lands, and of the reception of the people.

Elihu and Salome rejoiced to meet Jesus, and thanked the Father that they had lived to see His Glory in this messenger of love.

Jesus then went to the temple of the Sacred Brotherhood at Heliopolis, the city of the sun, and was admitted there.

His desire was to walk in every way of earth-life; to gain the heights that any man had gained; to experience the hardest tests, that he might be well fitted to assist his fellowmen. He took the vow of secret brotherhood.

Jesus was given his mystic name and number, Logos—Circle—Seven. The Circle is the symbol of the perfect man; seven is the number of the perfect man; Logos is the perfect word, that which creates, that which destroys, and that which saves.

The Master then bid Jesus to go forth and find his soul. Through revelation, Jesus found the Atman Self within his temple.

Then came the tempter with the subtle temptations of deception and hypocrisy; but Jesus was true to the brotherhood, to God, and to himself. The tempter left, and soon

38

the white-robed priest appeared, and led him to the hierophant, who placed within his hands a scroll, on which
was written, SINCERITY.

Then came other experiences that test the carnal man;
the tests of prejudice and treachery; but Jesus was loyal
and true; he was not deceived by these illusive foes, and
again a scroll was placed within his hands, on it was
written, JUSTICE.

After seven days Jesus was taken to the Hall of Fame.
He was entranced with the beauty of his surroundings and
with the works of master minds; the paintings and the
works of art. Soon a priest approached him saying: "Behold the glory of this place! My brother, you are highly
blest. Few men of earth, so young, have reached such
heights of fame. Now if you do not waste your life in
search of hidden things that men can never comprehend,
you may be founder of a school that will insure you endless fame. I would advise you to renounce uncertain things
and choose the course that leads to certain fame." Jesus
wrestled with his lower self for forty days; for ambition
was a mighty foe to fight; but faith rose triumphant. Jesus
saw beyond the illusion of the honor, wealth and fame of
carnal man; and with his eyes to heaven he prayed: "My
Father-God, I thank thee for this hour. I ask not for the
glory of thyself; I fain would be a keeper of thy temple
gates, and serve my brother man."

The white-robed hierophant placed within his hands
a scroll on which was written, FAITH. Jesus bowed his
head in humble thanks.

After some days had passed, a guide led Jesus to the
Hall of Mirth. Here were men and women gaily clad,
feasting, and dancing, and surrounded with the things
that bring the carnal sense of joy.. He watched them
silently for a time, and was invited to join them in their
mirth; but as he gazed upon the throng, he saw traces of
sin and want upon many faces. He turned from the revelry
to be of service to those he saw in need.

Jesus was victor over selfish self, and in his hands a

scroll was placed upon which was written, PHILAN-
THROPY.

Then after forty days had passed, came the tests that
cause the weak to fear, (the psychic forces that play upon
the mind of man) to test his strength to master them.
Jesus was not enmeshed in these illusive realms. He arose,
and with power from within he dispersed the phantoms,
and gained victory over fear; and he was given a scroll on
which HEROISM was written.

When Jesus had attained the victory over fear, he was
entitled to enter the Beauty Parlors of the temple of the
sun, where few students were admitted. Here in this place
of beauty, he saw a maiden fair to look upon, who played
upon a harp. She sang, and Jesus had not heard such music
nor seen such beauty. For many days the maiden and her
song filled his mind. At last he realized that he was sent
to demonstrate universal love, that is divine. He conquered
human love. The great bells of the temple rang, the grotto
blazed with light, the hierophant hailed this victory, and
placed within Jesus' hand a scroll on which was written, LOVE DIVINE. Together they passed from the
grotto of the beautiful. A feast was served in the banquet
hall, and Jesus was the honored guest.

Jesus was then taken as a private pupil of the hierophant, and was taught the mysteries of Egypt.

He learned the mystic lore of Egypt, the mysteries of
life and death, and of the worlds beyond the circle of the
Sun. He then went into the chamber of the Dead, to
learn the ancient methods of preserving from decay the
bodies of the dead. He met those in grief who came with
the bodies of their dead, and gave comfort to those who
did not comprehend eternal life. He gave the truth regarding death.

One day he met a child who had come with others,
and the body of her dead mother. She saw a wounded
bird and stopped to care for it. Jesus asked her why she
left her mother to tend the wounded bird, and the child
replied: "This lifeless body needs no help from me; but

I can help while yet life is; my mother taught me this."
She said: "Tears flow from hearts of flesh; the spirit
never weeps; and I am longing for the day when I will
walk in light, where tears are wiped away. My mother
taught that all emotions are the sprays that rise from
human loves, and hopes, and fears; that perfect bliss can
not be ours till we have conquered these." Jesus reverent-
ly bowed his head in the presence of this child.

When his work in the Chamber of the Dead was finished, Jesus stood in the temple purple room, before the
hierophant. He was clothed in purple robes; and all the
brothers stood. The hierophant arose, and said: "This is
a royal day for all the hosts of Israel. In honor of their
chosen son we celebrate the great Passover Feast," and then
he said to Jesus: "Brother, man, most excellent of men, in
all the temple tests you have won out. Six times before
the bar of right you have been judged; six times you have
received the highest honors man can give; and now you
stand prepared to take the last degree. Upon your brow I
place this diadem, and in the Great Lodge of the heavens
and earth you are, THE CHRIST. This is your great
Passover rite. You are neophyte no more; but now a
master. Now man can do no more; but God will speak,
and will confirm your title and degree. Go on your way,
for you must preach the gospel of good will to men and
peace on earth; must open up the prison doors, and set the
captives free."

And while the hierophant yet spoke the temple bells
rang out; a pure white dove descended from above and sat
on Jesus' head.

And then a voice that shook the very temple said:
THIS IS THE CHRIST; and every living creature said:
AMEN.

The great doors of the temple swung ajar; the Logos
journeyed on his way a conqueror.

*   *   *   *

(This great reward is for all upon the sacred path, who live the life of purity and service in consecration to the One Eternal God.)

PART TWO

THE SEVEN SAGES OF THE WORLD

In every age since time began, seven sages have lived. At the beginning of the Piscean age, seven sages met in Alexandria in Philo's home, to discuss the needs of all the people and to formulate the laws, religious postulates, and plans best suited to the coming age.

From China, Meng-ste came; from India, Vidiyapati; from Persia, Kaspar; from Greece, Apollo; Matheno from Egypt; and Philo was the Hebrew sage.

They sat in silence seven days, and then discussed the needs of their people. As they spoke, the council chamber door was opened and the Logos stood among the sages of the world. They sat again in silence seven days.

Then together they read the book of life, which contains the story of the life of man. As they read the past events, they saw the needs of future time. Each sage in turn wrote a postulate; and on these seven postulates the worship of the coming age would rest.

Then Meng-ste said: "The Holy One has sent to us a man illumined by the efforts of unnumbered years, to lead the thoughts of men. This man, approved by all the master minds of heaven and earth, this man from Galilee, this Jesus, chief of all the sages of the world, we gladly recognize. In recognition of this wisdom that he brings to men, we crown him with the lotus wreath. We send him forth with all the blessings of the seven sages of the world."

Then all the sages laid their hands on Jesus' head, and said with one accord, Praise God! For wisdom, honor, glory, power, riches, blessing, strength, are yours, O Christ, forever more.

After seven days of silence Jesus addressed the sages. He

said: "In taking up the work assigned for me to do I am full conscious of the perils of the way; the cup will be a bitter one to drink and human nature well might shrink. But I have lost my will in that of Holy Breath, and so I go my way to speak and act as I am moved to speak and act by Holy Breath."

He said that he would select twelve men of low estate, and these would represent the Model Church; that he would make a pattern of the church that was to be, and on the postulate that Love is son of God; and that he had come to manifest that Love, the Model Church would stand. He added: "My own kindred in the flesh will comprehend but little of my mission to the world. They will spurn me, scorn my work, accuse me falsely, bind me, take me to the judgment seat of carnal man, who will convict me and slay me upon the cross. But men can never slay the truth; though banished, it will come again in greater power; for truth will subjugate the world. The Model Church will stand, though man will prostitute its sacred laws, symbolic rites, and forms, for selfish ends, and make it but an outward show; the few will find through it the kingdom of the soul. And when the better age shall come the Universal Church will stand upon the seven postulates, and will be built according to the pattern given. The kingdom of the soul shall be established on the seven hills, in the name of our Father-God. The Prince of Peace will take his seat upon the throne of power; the Triune God will then be the All in All. (Aquarian Gospel, Chapter 47-60 in part.)

* * * *

In the new age in which we are living, the Universal Church is being established. It will stand as Jesus told the seven sages in Alexandria. The kingdom of the soul, which is Aum, will be established upon the earth. Man will rise upon the seven rungs of the ladder which reaches from carnality into the light of Aum.

Every soul that has wandered in consciousness from this presence is destined to return again.

Atman, the divine self, has never lost the memory of this presence. Desire expressed, he turned away from the light within. Gradually his vibrations lowered from the divine state of consciousness until he became clothed with the garments of the world, and entangled within the carnal dream. Thus he has lived in a seeming separate state for ages; but in the eternal law of God the time arrives, when each soul awakens from the dream; he hears the Father's call, and turns to retrace his steps to his Father's house.

None other than the path of Christ will lead him there. In Flashlights of Truth, page 116-118, we read: "When man awakens, even slightly, from the deep sleep of the Adam dream and begins to perceive the plan of the Infinite, he will soon see how dim his light is; and, if he desires more light, he will soon find more light shining upon the upward way."

"Jesus Christ is the Light of the World. He is the pattern—man. When man awakens to the Light in Jesus' message, man will endeavor to bring forth the pattern in himself. At first he may express it feebly; but, as his endeavors are more intelligently carried forth, his expression will become more perfect, until he comes into the full consciousness of the Christ. He then will express the pattern—man in his body, until he becomes the Glorified Body of the Christ."

—Aum—is the key.—

LESSON V.

JOHN'S MINISTRY AS HARBINGER
BEGINNING OF JESUS' MINISTRY

WHEN John had completed his studies in the Egyptian schools, he returned to Hebron; and, later made his home in David's cave in the wilderness, where Matheno taught him years before. He clothed himself with skins of beasts; and ate carobs, honey, nuts, a n d fruit. He lived as a hermit in this wilderness until he reached thirty years of age. Then he went to Jerusalem and sat in silence seven days in the market place. Multitudes came to see the hermit of the hills, as he was called; but none asked him who he was.

After his fast he stood among the people, and proclaimed the coming of the Prince of Peace. He said: "Prepare, O Israel, prepare to meet your king." Then he disappeared. All Jerusalem was in excitement. The rulers sent couriers forth to John to learn about the coming king; but none could find him.

After certain days he stood again in the market place, and said: "Be not disturbed, you rulers of the state; the coming king is no antagonist; he seeks no place on any earthly throne; he comes the Prince of Peace, the king of righteousness and love; his kingdom is within the soul. The eyes of men shall see it not, and none can enter but the pure in heart. Prepare, O Israel, prepare to meet your king."

Then John stood in the temple at Jerusalem, and told the people to turn from their evil ways or God would turn from them. He told them of their injustice to the poor, and that their places set aside for prayer were dens for thieves.

The priests, the doctors, and scribes were in a rage, and were intent to do him harm; but the common people stood in his defense.

When he came again the chief priests and scribes asked the meaning of his words, and who had sent him with his message to Israel. John replied: "I am the voice of one who cries out in the wilderness, Prepare the way, make straight the paths, for, lo, the Prince of Peace will come to rule in love. Your prophet Malachi wrote down the words of God: And I will send Elijah unto you before the retribution day shall come, to turn again the hearts of men to God."

John said: "Reform, O Israel, reform; prepare to meet your king."

Before he left the temple he told the people that in seven days he would stand at Gilgal, by the Jordan ford. He left the temple to enter it no more, and went to the home of Lazarus, his kin, in Bethany. He remained with Lazarus and his sisters certain days, and in honor of the Nazarite a feast was spread and all the people stood about the board.

The chief men of Bethany offered John a cup of sparkling wine. John took it, and held it high, and said: "Wine makes glad the carnal heart, and it makes sad the human soul; it plunges deep in bitterness and gall the deathless spirit of the man. I took the vow of Nazar when a child, and not a drop has ever passed my lips. And if you would make glad the coming king, then shun the cup as you would shun a deadly thing."

Then John went down to Jericho; and, when the time was due, he went to the Jordan ford. He met the multitudes who came, and he said: "Come unto me, and in the waters of this stream be washed, symbolic of the inner cleansing of the soul." And many came, confessed their sins, and they were washed. And then he went again to Bethany to teach. John pleaded for purity and righteousness, and when he saw the Pharisees and Sadducees who

came without contrition in their hearts, he said to them:
"Go to, and do the things that prove repentance genuine."
To the people he said: "Accept the ministry of helpfulness for all mankind, and spend not upon your selfish
selves all that you have." For months he worked among
the people, and many of the Jews who were waiting for
the Christ to come regarded John as Christ. To their
questions he replied: "In water I do cleanse, symbolic of
the cleansing of the soul; but, when he comes who is to
come, lo, he will cleanse in Holy Breath, and purify in
fire. His fan is in his hand, and he will separate the wheat
and chaff; will throw the chaff away, but garner every
grain of wheat. This is the Christ. Behold he comes!
And he will walk with you, and you will know him not.
He is the king; the latchet of his shoes I am not worthy
to unloose."

From Galilee, Jesus and the multitudes went to the
Jordan ford, where John had returned to preach. When
Jesus saw his harbinger, he said: "Behold the man of
God! Behold the greatest of the Seers! Behold, Elijah has
returned. Behold the messenger whom God has sent to
open up the way! The kingdom is at hand."

And when John saw Jesus and the throng, he said:
"Behold the king who cometh in the name of God."

Jesus asked to be washed, as he was a pattern for all
men who must be washed, symbolic of the cleansing of
the soul. He said: "What I bid them to do, that I must
do. This washing we establish as a rite—baptism rite it
shall be called." Then John led Jesus into the river at
the ford, and baptized him in the sacred name of him who
sent him to manifest the Christ to men. A dove descended
from above, and sat on Jesus' head. A voice from heaven
said: "This is the well-beloved son of God, the Christ,
the love of God made manifest." (Aquarian Gospel,
Chapter 64 in part.)

Jesus went his way. Many who followed were baptized by the harbinger.

Before Jesus entered upon his ministry he went into the wilderness for forty days to commune with God.

The tempter came, and said: "If you be Son of God, command these stones to turn to bread." Jesus knew that it would not be proof of his Messiahship if he turned the stones to bread; for black magicians, who know not God, do many works. He said: "My words and deeds in all the walks of life shall be the proof of my Messiahship." Again the tempter said: "If you will go into Jerusalem, and from the temple pinnacle cast down yourself to earth, the people will believe that you are the Messiah sent from God." Jesus said: "I may not tempt the Lord, my God."

Then the tempter said: "Look forth upon the world; behold its honor and its fame! Behold its pleasures and its wealth! If you will give your life for these they shall be yours."

Jesus' heart was fixed. These temptations could not turn him from his call, and when he left the wilderness he was in the consciousness of Holy Breath.

He went to John, and six of John's disciples followed him. They sought to know what they must do to follow in his path. Jesus said: "He who would follow me must give up all the cravings of the self and lose his life in saving life. I came to save the lost, and man is saved when he is rescued from himself." Peter, one of the six disciples said: "I will leave all, and follow where you lead." The others believed that Jesus had the truth, and Jesus and the six disciples sat long in silence.

Next day Jesus stood with John beside the ford. He told the people that the great key-keeper of the age was in their midst; that he had turned the key, and the gates were open for all who would greet the king. He said: "O men of Israel, take heed of what this prophet has to say! Be strong in mind; be pure in heart; be vigilant in helpfulness; the kingdom is at hand." He then took his disciples to Bethany and abode with Lazarus many days.

The people of Bethany came to hear Jesus speak. He

told them, as he stood in their midst, that Christ was universal love; and that Christ would be formed in every one of them, as it was formed in him, when they had purified their hearts.

The people asked how they might purify their bodies to make it a fit abiding place for the king. And Jesus said: "Each must study for himself how he can best transmute his tendency to evil things to that of righteousness and love." This rule will give the best results: "Do unto other men what you would have them do to you."

Then Jesus went to Jerusalem. His six disciples and many of the people followed him. When he reached the temple court he opened a book, and read: "Behold, I send my messenger, and he will pave the way; and Christ, for whom you wait, will come unto his temple unannounced. Behold, for he will come, says God, the Lord of hosts." He then went to Nazareth with his disciples to his mother's home. He did not teach in Nazareth. To those that gathered about, he said: "A prophet has no honor in his native town, among his kin. I will not speak in Nazareth until the words I speak and works I do in other towns have won the faith of men."

In Cana, Galilee, Jesus manifested his divine power in turning water into wine at a wedding feast. Understanding the law of vibration he brought forth that which was desired.

In Capernaum, he taught the difference between Christ, the king within, and the king who wears the royal robe and sits upon a throne in the outer world. He said: "The carnal man beholds the outer man which is the temple of the king, and worships at his shrine. The man of God is pure in heart; he sees the king; he sees with eyes of soul. And when he rises to the plane of Christine consciousness, he knows that he himself is king, is love, is Christ; and so, is son of God."

During the Jewish paschal-feast time in Jerusalem, Jesus abode with Jude, a Sadducee. When he entered the temple he saw the money changers selling lambs for sacrifice. He drove them out, unloosed the lambs, and set the birds in cages free. To the priests he said: "Behold, for paltry gain you have sold out the temple of the Lord." The rulers said to Jesus: "Man, if you be king or Christ, then show us signs." Jesus said: "The signs of my messiahship will follow me in words and deeds. And you may tear this temple down (and you will tear it down) and in three days it will be built again more glorious than before." He meant that they might take his life, tear down his body, temple of the Holy Breath, and he would rise again. They laughed, and would have driven him away, but Philo, who had come from Egypt, said: "Be not hasty, men; just wait, and you will have the proofs of his messiahship. I have seen him touch the sick, and they were healed; I have heard him speak, and all the winds were still; he stands a sage above the sages of the world."

Then Jesus said: "Prepare, O Israel, prepare to meet your king! But you can never see the king while you press sin as such a precious idol to your hearts. The King is God; the pure in heart alone can see the face of God, and live. Our Father-God is King. I am the candle of the Lord aflame to light the way; and while you have the light, walk in the light."

Next day Jesus defined Messiahship. He said: "Messiah is one sent from God to save the lost. In first of every age Messiah comes to light the way; to heal the broken hearts; to set the prisoners free. Messiah and the Christ are One."

On the Sabbath day he healed the sick, and restored to life a child who had been drowned. He called aloud unto the soul that had gone out of the child's body, and it returned. (The soul is conscious life.) He cared for a wounded dog, and fed and clothed a little boy. To those who followed him the master said: "If man would gain his lost estate he must respect the brotherhood of life. Whoever is not kind to every form of life—to man, to beast, to bird, and creeping thing—can not expect the blessings of the Holy One; for, as we give, so God will give to us."

Nicodemus, a ruler of the Jews, heard Jesus speak, and saw the master's signet in his face. He went to talk with him at the home of Jude at night. He greeted Jesus as they met, as a teacher come from God.

Jesus said to Nicodemus: "Except a man be born again he cannot see the king; he cannot comprehend the words I speak. To Nicodemus' question: "How can a man be born again?" Jesus replied: "The birth of which I speak is not the birth of flesh. Except a man be born of water and the Holy Breath, he cannot come into the kingdom of the Holy One. That which is born of flesh is flesh; that which is born of Holy Breath is child of God."

The kingdom of the soul can not be comprehended by the intellect of man. Its recognition is the work of the inner consciousness. As Moses in the wilderness raised up the serpent for the healing of the flesh, so the son of man must be raised up, that all men bitten by the serpent of the dust, the serpent of the carnal life, may live. For God so loved the world that he sent forth his only son to be raised up that men may see the light of God. God did not send his son to judge the world; he sent him forth to save the world; to bring men to the light. And every one who loves the truth comes to the light; he does not fear to have his works made manifest.

The light had come; Nicodemus went his way; he knew the meaning of the birth of Holy Breath; he felt the presence of the spirit in his soul. (Aquarian Gospel, 61-75 in part.)

*   *   *   *

Man may be highly illumined intellectually concerning spiritual things; yet to know the truth as Jesus Christ taught and lived it requires the spiritual light of the New Birth and this is a gift from God, and is conferred upon him in answer to prayer.

Aum is the One Universal Spirit. When man is born

again a ray of the Supreme Spirit enters in and abides in form in him.

In Flashlights of Truth, we read: "Communion with God is the central point around which revolves all lesser details in man's work-shop (his mind and heart). 'Alone with God,' in At-one-ment with God! Man may know of his at-one-ment with God in theory; but it will not become a reality to him until he has come to the New Birth, and has entered into the Christ Consciousness; and, as he advances in this consciousness, man can speak as Jesus spoke, his words being filled with power."

"The New Birth takes place when man has reached the border line of enlightenment. Then He, the Spirit of Truth, the comforter within sent from God, will teach and lead the new-born one into all truth, into Enlighten-ment. He then recognizes the truth of his being, that he, too, is a son of the Living God, and that Jesus Christ is an Elder Brother."

Lesson VI.

THE MINISTRY OF JESUS AND JOHN
Continued

JESUS CALLS HIS DISCIPLES

JESUS tarried in Jerusalem many days. The common people followed him and he taught and healed the sick.

He then went to Bethlehem, and abode in the home where he was cradled when a babe.

The shepherds came from near and far when they heard that Jesus had come to Bethlehem, and Jesus talked with them of love and peace; he said: "Once again the Prince of Peace has come, and from these blessed hills he goes again to fight, and he is clothed in white; his shield is faith; his helmet innocence; his breath is love; his watchword peace."

Again the hills were clothed with light; and messengers again exclaimed: "Peace, peace on earth, good will to men."

Jesus taught and healed the sick, and revealed the mysteries of the kingdom of the Holy One. And then he went to Hebron and taught for seven days.

In Bethany, at Lazarus' home he taught the multitudes. When in the evening they had gone, he talked with Lazarus and his sisters, Mary, Ruth and Martha.

In Jericho he healed the sick, and then went to the Jordan ford where John was teaching. He led his six disciples into the ford, and in the name of Christ he baptized them; he said: "As I baptize you in the name of Christ, so you shall, in that sacred name, baptize all men and women who confess their faith in Christ, and shall renounce their sins." Multitudes came, renounced their sins, confessed their faith in Christ, and were baptized.

53

At Salim Springs, John, the harbinger, went next to preach. He told the multitudes that Jesus, who was preaching at the Jordan ford, had been subjected to the hardest tests of human life; that he had conquered all the appetites and passions of the carnal man; that love divine abode in him; that he was the pattern for the race; and that all could see, in Jesus, what they would be when they had conquered self.

John said: "I have washed the bodies of the people who have turned from sin; but Jesus bathes forever in the living waters of Holy Breath," and that Jesus came to bring the savior of the world to men; that Love was savior of the world.

Lamaas, the priest of Brahm from the temple Jagannath in India, came to Jesus as he taught beside the ford. Jesus greeted Lamaas, saying: "Behold the Star of India." And Lamaas said: "Behold the sun of righteousness!"

Lamaas had talked with John at Salim Springs. John told Lamaas of the divine mission of Jesus, the Christ, and said: "The groves of nature are his synagogues; and his forum is the world."

And Lamaas confessed his faith in Christ, and followed Jesus and the six disciples unto Galilee.

At Sychar, in Samaria, Jesus sat alone beside Jacob's well. A woman from Samaria came for water. Jesus asked her for a drink. She said: "Do you not know that there is enmity between Samaritans and Jews? They traffic not; then why ask me the favor of a drink?" Jesus said: "I recognize the brotherhood of life; Samaritans are just as dear to me as Jews." He told her of the living water which he brought. He said: "Lo, everyone who drinks from Jacob's well will thirst again; but they who drink the water that I give, will never thirst again; for they themselves become a well, and from their inner parts the sparkling waters bubble up into eternal life." He told her that he had come to break away the wall that separates the sons of men; that the hour had come when men must worship God within the temple of the heart; that God is

Spirit, and they who worship him must worship him in spirit and in truth.

The woman said: "We know that, when Messiah comes, he will lead us in the ways of truth." And Jesus said: "Behold, the Christ has come. Messiah speaks to you."

Then in the market place in Sychar, Jesus taught, and cast an evil spirit out of one obsessed, and healed the sick. The rulers and priests were much disturbed; they thought that Jesus had come to stir up strife. Jesus told them he was the one who, as their prophet had foretold, would come; that he had come to help and not to hinder them; and he taught them of the brotherhood of man.

In the city of Samaria the multitudes begged the Christines to tarry; and Jesus went to the synagogue. He opened up the book of Moses, and read: "In thee and all thy seed shall all the nations of the earth be blessed." He said: "We are his seed, but not a tithe of the great work that we were called to do has yet been done. The Lord of hosts has set the Israelites apart to teach the unity of God and man, but one can never teach that which he does not demonstrate in life." To the ruler and the priests, he said: "All men are looking unto you for guidance in the ways of life; example is another name for priest; so, what you would that people should be, that you must be."

When Jesus left the synagogue he went up to the sacred grove to pray. While he sat there a soul spoke to his soul imploring help. It was a dying woman who had heard that Jesus was a man of God. She called to him and instantly she arose. Jesus filled the dying one with life. He raised the vibration of her body from disease to that of health and life. Later, Jesus walked with the disciples to Nazareth.

In the city of Tiberius on the shores of Galilee, Herod Antipas lived with his wife Herodias.

John was teaching the people by the sea of Galilee. He rebuked Herod and his wife for their wickedness. Herodias became enraged, and caused Herod to cast John in a dungeon by the Bitter Sea. John's followers were restrained from teaching in the public halls.

Friends of Jesus, hearing the fate of John, implored him not to remain in Galilee.

But Jesus said: "I have no need of fear, my time is not yet come; no man can stay me till my work is done, and when my work is done the rulers will do to me what they have done to John, and more." Of John he said: "Behold, yon stalk of wheat! When it has brought the grain to perfectness, it is of no more worth; it falls, becoming part of earth again from which it came. John is a stalk of golden wheat; he brought unto maturity the richest grain of all the earth; his work is done. If he had said another word it might have marred the symmetry of what is now a noble life. These events are part of God's own plan. The innocent will suffer while the wicked are in power; but woe to them who cause the innocents to suffer."

In Nazareth at the synagogue Jesus told the people gathered there, that the year of jubilee was at hand, and the scriptures would be fulfilled before their eyes. He said: "The Spirit of the Lord has overshadowed me; He has anointed me to preach the gospel to the poor; to set the captives free; to open sightless eyes; to bring relief to those oppressed and bruised."

The people said: "Do here among your kindred all the mighty works that you have done in other towns." Jesus answered: "No prophet is received with honor in his native land; and prophets are not sent to every one. You have no faith; you seek for signs to satisfy your curious whims; you shall not see till you open up your eyes of faith."

The people were enraged at Jesus' words, they rushed upon him, bound him, and would have thrown him from a precipice; but, when they thought they held him fast, he disappeared. Later, they found him teaching in the synagogue in Nazareth.

Then Jesus and his disciples went to Cana. From

Capernaum came a nobleman who had faith in Jesus'
power to heal. His son was very ill. He asked Jesus to go
to Capernaum, and save his son; but Jesus stood awhile
in silence, and then he said: "Your faith has proved a
healing balm; your son is well." The man believed, and
went his way. His son was well.

Jesus did not remain long in Cana. He went unto
Capernaum with his disciples. There he secured a spacious
home for his mother and himself, and to provide a place
where his disciples could meet and hear his message. His
disciples called this home, "The School of Christ." Here
Jesus told them that the gospel of the Christ must be proclaimed to all the world. He said: "I am the vine; twelve
men shall be the stock, and these shall send forth branches
everywhere; and from among the people who have followed me, the Holy Breath will call the twelve. Go, now,
and do your work as you have done your work; but listen
for the call." The disciples left and Jesus went to the
Hammoth hills and communed three days with the Silent
Brotherhood. Then in the power of Holy Breath he went
beside the sea of Galilee. There he walked, and multitudes followed him.

Peter and his brother were in their fishing boats waiting for their nets to be repaired. Jesus stepped into the
boat and spoke to the multitude saying: "Isaiah, prophet
of the Lord of hosts, looked forward, and he saw this
day; he saw the people standing by the sea, and he exclaimed: "The land of Zebulon and Naphtali, land beyond the Jordan and toward the sea, the Gentile Galilee,
the people were in darkness, knowing not the way; but,
lo, they saw the Day Star rise; a light streamed forth;
they saw the way of life; they walked therein."

Then Jesus said to Peter: "Bring your nets aboard,
and put out in the deep." Peter responded in a faithless
way, saying: "Andrew and I have toiled all night, and
taken naught." Jesus said: "Cast your net upon the right
side of the boat." The net was filled. Peter called to
James and John, who were standing near, for help; and

they drew in the heavy catch. Jesus said: "Behold the catch! from henceforth you shall fish no more for fish; you shall cast forth the Christine net into the sea of human life, upon the right side of the boat; you shall ensnare the multitudes to holiness and blessedness and peace."

When they reached the shore he said to Peter, Andrew, James, and John: "You, fishermen of Galilee, the masters have a mighty work for us to do; I go, and you may follow me." Walking along the shore he saw Philip and Nathanael, and said to them: "You, teachers of Bethsaida, who long have taught the people Greek philosophy, the masters have a higher work for you and me to do; I go, and you may follow me."

Then Jesus saw Matthew, the officer in charge of the tribute house, a man of wealth and culture. He said to him: "Hail, Matthew, trusted servant of the Cæsars, hail! the masters call us to the tribute house of souls; I go, and you may follow me." Then to Judas, employed at the tribute house he said: "Stay your work; the masters call us to a duty in the saving-bank of souls. I go, and you may follow." Jesus then met a lawyer who had come to study at the school of Christ. Thomas was his name. To him Jesus said: "The masters have a need of men who can interpret law; I go, and you may follow me." In the evening he saw his kindred, James and Jude, who had worked with him as carpenters. He said: "The masters call us now to aid in building homes for souls; homes built without the sound of hammer, ax, or saw; I go, and you may follow me." Next day Jesus sent a message to Simon, a strict exponent of the Jewish law. The message said: "The masters call for men to demonstrate the faith of Abraham; I go, and you may follow me."

These twelve disciples, whom Jesus called, met before the Sabbath day at Jesus' home. They were all in one accord, and Jesus said to them: "This is the day to consecrate yourselves unto the work of God; so let us pray." Together they prayed in the inner chamber of the soul and a light more brilliant than the sun filled the room; a tongue of flame rose high from each disciple's head, and each one heard the still small voice speak the sacred name of God. Jesus said to them: "By this omnific Word you may control the elements, and all the powers of the air; and when you speak this Word within your souls, you have the keys to life and death; of things that are; of things that were; of things that are to be. Behold, you are the twelve great branches of the Christine vine; the twelve foundation stones; the twelve apostles of the Christ. As lambs I send you forth among wild beasts; but the omnific Word will be your buckler and your shield."

The air was filled with song, and every living creature seemed to say: "Praise God!" Amen! (Aquarian Gospel, 76:89 in part.)

The omnific Word is Aum, the Eternal One, the Father-God, the Source. It is the Spirit-Substance, the Essence from whence all manifests came forth, and to whom all are destined to return again. Aum is the Kingdom. Aum is Peace, Life, Love, Intelligence; Light, Power and Harmony. Aum is limitless. It is the All in All, the Omnipresence, the Living God.

LESSON VII.

JESUS' TEACHING AND MINISTRY.
Continued

JESUS and his twelve disciples went to the synagogue on the following Sabbath day, and Jesus taught the people. They said: "He teaches as a man who knows and has authority to speak."

A man obsessed with evil spirits came to the synagogue, and when they saw the Master they knew him, and they said: "You son of God, why are you here? Would you destroy us by the Word before our time? We would have naught to do with you; let us alone." Jesus said to them: "By the omnific Word I speak; come out: torment this man no more; go to your place." The unclean spirits threw the man upon the floor, and with a fiendish cry they went away. Jesus lifted up the man, and said: "If you will keep your mind fully occupied with good, the evil spirits can not find a place to stay: they only come to empty heads and hearts."

Many were astonished at Jesus' words and power.

He left the synagogue with Peter, Andrew, James, and John; and went to Peter's home. He healed one near of kin and others who were brought to him, and then he disappeared. Later, Peter, James, and John found him out on the Hammoth hills.

With his twelve disciples Jesus went to Bethsaida, and taught. Multitudes came; confessed their sins, and were baptized. The Christines went through all the towns of Galilee; and Jesus taught, healed the sick, and drove unclean spirits out of those obsessed. At Tiberius, a leper who believed that Jesus could make him clean, was healed. The leper was wild with joy; and, in the marts of trade

60

and everywhere, told what was done. Then throngs pressed hard upon Jesus and the twelve, imploring to be healed.

The Christines returned to Capernaum as the Jewish festival drew near. There, in his home, Jesus healed many. A palsied man who could not enter through the crowded door was taken by four men to the roof, and let down before the Master's face. Seeing their faith, he said to the palsied man: "Be of good cheer, your sins are all forgiven." (Jesus taught that infirmity was the paying up of debts, and that when they were all paid up, sins were blotted out.) To the palsied man he said: "Arise, take up your bed and go your way." The man arose, took up his bed, and went his way. The people who saw these works of Jesus said: "This is a day we never can forget, we have seen wondrous things to-day."

Early on the Sabbath day Jesus and the twelve went through the sheep-gate to Jerusalem. The healing fountain of Bethesda, near the gate, was thronged with people who were sick. Jesus saw a man who had been stricken many years. He said to him: "My brother, man, would you be healed?" He said: "I earnestly desire to be healed." Jesus told him that the fount of health was in his soul; it had a door locked fast; the key was faith; and Jesus said: "Do you believe what I have said? According to your faith it shall be done. Arise, take up your bed, and walk." The people asked the man who had made him whole. The man replied: "A stranger at the pool just spoke a word, and I was well."

In the temple Jesus told the people that all men were the sons of God; that if they lived a holy life, they would always be at home with God. He said: "You, men of Israel, hear! You live in death; you are locked up within the tomb. But all will some day hear the voice of God, made plain by voice of man, and live. You will know that you are sons of God; and, by the sacred word, may do the works of God." Thus Jesus taught all people of the Fatherhood of God and of the brotherhood of man.

Lazarus was at the feast, and Jesus and the twelve went to his home in Bethany. There Lazarus and his sisters spread a feast. Ruth and Asher came from Jericho. Asher had been hostile to the Christ; but, later, he believed on him. While the guests were seated they heard the cry: "The village is afire." They rushed out, and saw the homes of many neighbors burning. A mother called for one to save her child in an upper room.

Jesus said: "Peace, peace, be still!" He walked through flame and smoke, and in a moment he brought the child unharmed. He raised his hand and rebuked the spirits of the fire, and commanded them to cease their awful work, and be at rest. The fire ceased to burn. To the multitudes who saw him control the fire, Jesus said: "When man comes to himself, and comprehends the fact that he is son of God, and knows that in himself lies all the powers of God, he is a Master; and all the elements will hear his voice, and gladly do his will."

Later, as Jesus sat with Lazarus and his guests, a little child came in, and asked Jesus if he would go with her to her home, and touch her father's heart. She said: "He is a drunken man, and squanders every cent for drink." Jesus went to the wretched home, and found the drunken man. He took him by the hand, and raised him up, and said: "My brother, man, made in the image of our Father-God, will you arise and come with me?" The man arose, and walked with Jesus, and saw the needs of many people. A spark of hope within the man was fanned into a flame. He called for help, and many came, and soon the homes were built again. The man was saved, and no one ever again said a word about neglect or drunkenness, nor urged him to reform.

The Christines returned to Capernaum, and Jesus taught in the synagogue on the Sabbath day, and healed a follower who had a withered hand. The Scribes and Pharisees were filled with rage. They called a secret council to plot and plan to bring about his death. They did not publicly accuse Jesus, because the multitudes stood in his defense.

Next morning Jesus took the twelve to a mountain near the sea, and there he taught them how to pray. He said: "Prayer is the deep communion of the soul with God, when you pray, go to the closet of your soul; close all the doors, and in the holy silence pray. A fast, is deed of soul; and, like a prayer, it is a function of the silence of the soul." He said: "God never passes by unnoticed any prayer, or effort of the soul; He walks within the silence, and his benedictions rest on every effort of the soul." He gave them the model prayer (which is the Universal prayer). They reached the mountain top, and Jesus said to them: "Twelve pillars of the church, apostles of the Christ, light-bearers of the sun of life, and ministers of God to men: In just a little while you must go forth alone, and preach the gospel of the king, first to the Jews, and then to all the world. And you shall go, not with a scourge of cords to drive; you can not drive men to the king; but you shall go in love and helpfulness, and lead the way to right and light. Go forth, and say: The Kingdom is at hand."

Jesus pronounced the eight beatitudes and the eight woes. He encouraged the disciples to live within the Holy Breath. He said: "You are light; are called to light the world. A city on a hill cannot be hid; its lights are seen afar; and, while you stand upon the hills of life, men see your light, and imitate your works, and honor God. You are the lamps of God; you must not stand in the shade of earth illusions, but in the open, high upon the stand." He said: "I am not come to nullify the law, but to fulfill. Whoever disregards the law of God and teaches men to do the same, becomes a debtor unto God, and can not see his face until he has returned, and paid his debt by sacrifice of life. But he who harkens unto God, and keeps his law, and does his will on earth, shall rule with Christ."

He said: "The letter of the law deals with the acts of man; the spirit of the law takes note of his desires."

Jesus unfolded the spiritual meaning of the ten commandments given to Moses by Jehovah, which show the justice side of God. But the love of God made manifest brought mercy on the wings of Holy Breath. (He, Jesus, this Love made manifest, brought grace and truth through Christ.)

Wisdom is the counterpart of love, and upon the unity of God the law was built. In all the world Jehovah is Almighty God; and, that all men might be the substance, in his mercy, He commanded: "You shall seek no God but me." And man must worship Him in Spirit and in Truth. Man may not speak the name of God with carnal lips; with Holy Breath alone he may pronounce His Holy name.

In forming worlds God rested on the seventh day, and every seventh day is set apart as Sabbath day for men. This day is consecrated unto God; but man serves God by serving man.

The man who honors the Almighty and Omniscient God is blessed, and in the tables of the law we read: "Pay homage to your Father and your Mother of the race."

Man judges man in the letter of the law if he does a wrong; Spirit judges man if he desires to do a wrong. Throughout the commands Jesus gave the spirit of the law, and taught the golden rule. He said: "There are many men with seeming double hearts; men who would serve two masters at a time, two masters quite adverse; but no man can serve two masters at a time; men can not lay treasures up in heaven and in earth at once."

He said: "Fix not your hearts upon the things of earth; be anxious not about the things to eat, or drink, or wear. God cares for those who trust in Him and serve the race."

He told his disciples not to judge and condemn as they walked among men, but to show mercy and love; and, if they had not food for every soul, to ask in faith, and it would be given.

He said: "The way to perfect life few find at a time; it is a narrow way, it lies among the rocks and pitfalls

of the carnal life; but in the way there are no pitfalls
and no rocks. There is a way that leads to wretchedness
and want; it lies among the pleasure groves of carnal life.
It is the way of death."

He bade his disciples to build their lives upon the solid
rock of truth, that evil could not harm; and when he had
finished all his sayings on the mount, he and the twelve
returned unto Capernaum.

A Roman captain who had heard that Jesus healed
with the sacred word, sent word of his servant's illness,
and pleaded for Jesus' help. Jesus recognized the captain's faith, and went at once to heal the sick. The captain met him on the way, and said: "Lo, Lord, it is not
well that you should come into my house. I am not
worthy of the presence of a man of God. If you will
speak the Word, I know my servant will be well." Jesus
turned to those who followed him, and said: "Behold the
captain's faith; I have not seen such faith, no, not in
Israel." He said to the man: "Go on your way; according
to your faith so shall it be; your servant lives."

In Nain, the Christines saw a funeral pass. A mother
grieved for her only son. Jesus said to her: "Weep not,
I am the life; your son shall live." He touched the bier,
and said: "Young man, return." The soul returned; the
body of the dead was filled with life; the man sat up, and
spoke.

The Christines taught and healed the sick in all the
towns of Galilee, and then returned unto Capernaum.

In the morning hours Jesus taught the twelve apostles
and the foreign priests the secret things of God, that they
might teach the people how to live the holy life. He
taught them how to teach; of the trials of the way; and
how to live that they might conquer death. The other
hours of the day he gave to those who came to learn the
way of life and to be healed.

One day as Jesus looked upon the multitude that
pressed about for selfish gain, he saw men of learning, of
reputation and power; but they did not know the Christ.

Jesus looked to heaven, and said: "I thank thee, Holy One of heaven and earth, that while the light is hidden from the wise and great, it is revealed to babes."

He told the people that he brought them the wisdom from above, and said: "Come unto me all you who labor and pull heavy loads, and I will give you aid. Put on the yoke of Christ with me; it does not chafe; it is an easy yoke. Together we will pull the load of life with ease; and so rejoice."

Simon was a Pharisee. In Jesus' honor he prepared a feast. It was the custom of all loyal Jews to wash their hands and feet before a feast. Simon neglected this courtesy to his guest.

While they sat about the table, a woman came in unbidden. She had been healed by Jesus of obsessing spirits, and in her gratitude she stooped at Jesus' feet. She bathed them with her tears and wiped them with her hair, and then anointed them with costly ointment from an alabaster box.

Simon, misunderstanding, thought that Jesus was not a prophet, else he would not permit this woman's humble act of love. Jesus called Simon aside; knowing his thoughts, he said: "Which merits the greater praise, this woman or yourself? When I came in you gave me not a bowl of water to bathe my hands and feet. Now tell me, Simon, which of these, this woman or yourself, is worthy of most praise?" Simon did not answer.

Many wealthy women, among them Mary Magdalene, desired Jesus and the foreign masters to go into other towns of Galilee to preach, and to heal the people. They provided funds, and twenty-one went forth to preach the gospel, heal the sick, and raise the dead. Jesus worked from morn till night. He did not stop to eat or rest. Some became alarmed lest his strength should fail. He said to them: "I tell you, men, while I am giving out my strength unto these anxious, waiting throngs, I find myself at rest within the arms of God, whose blessed messengers bring down to me the bread of life."

Some believed that Jesus was a God; others saw in him a devil, and would destroy him; others were his friend or foe, as it suited them. Jesus said: "No man can serve two masters at a time. No one can be friend and foe at once. You, men, do not deceive yourselves in thought; your hearts are known. Hypocrisy will blight a soul as surely as the breath of Beelzebul. And if you sin against a son of man, you may be pardoned, and your guilt be cleansed by acts of kindness and of love; but if you sin against the Holy Breath by disregarding her when she would open up the doors of life for you, by closing up the windows of the soul when she would pour the light of love into your hearts, and cleanse them with the fires of God, your guilt shall not be blotted out in this or in the life to come; an opportunity has gone, to come no more; and you must wait until the ages roll again. I tell you, men, that you must give account to God for every idle word and every evil deed you do."

In Magdala by the sea, Jesus taught. He cast out spirits from one obsessed, and opened up his eyes and ears. This was the greatest work the Pharisees had seen. They were full of jealous rage, and sought to condemn Jesus by likening his works to the works of black magicians of Moses' day. Jesus knew their thoughts. He said: "If Satan casts the devil out, how can his kingdom stand? But if I, in the holy name of God, cast devils out, and make the lame to walk, the deaf to hear, the dumb to speak, has not God's kingdom come to you?"

A Pharisee stood forth among the multitude and said to Jesus: "Sir, we would have you demonstrate. If you are truly Christ who was to come, then you can surely do what black magicians can not do." Jesus said: "No black magician ever lived a holy life; you have a demonstration of the Christ life every day; you cry phenomena! Show us a sign, and then we will believe. I was not sent to earth to buy up faith as men buy fish and fruit and rubbish in the streets. Faith is not something you can buy with coin; it is not something you can sell for gold. But

I will give to all the world one sign as surety that the Christ abides with me. The son of man will spend three days and nights within the heart of earth, and then come forth again, and men will see and know. Behold, the light may be so bright that man can not see anything. The spirit light has shown so brightly over Galilee that you who hear me now are blind. The Queen of Sheba sat in darkest night, and still she yearned for light. She came to hear the words of wisdom from the lips of Solomon, and she believed. A greater far than Solomon is here; the Christ is here; the Day Star has arisen, and you reject the light."

"Behold, for every one to whom I speak has in him all the fires of God; but they are lying dead. Holy Breath can raise the ethers of the fires to light in none but hearts of purity and love. Hear then, you, men of Galilee, make pure the heart; admit the Holy Breath; and then your bodies will be full of light. And, like a city on a hill, your light will shine afar, and thus your light may light the way for other men." (Aquarian Gospel, Chapters 90-107 in part.)

*   *   *   *

Jesus Christ's life stands out strong and clear in the foreground of the past centuries above all others, as we read the recorded history of mankind. He gave the message which, when understood, will enable man to know that he is in the boundless freedom of the son of God and forever at-one with God. Jesus being the pattern man, his life from day to day is an example for all men as they walk upon the Christ path. (Flashlights of Truth.)

Lesson VIII.

JESUS' TEACHING AND MINISTRY,
Continued

JESUS SENDS THE DISCIPLES AND FOREIGN MASTERS FORTH TO PREACH

AT a feast given by a wealthy Pharisee, Jesus exposed the hypocrisy of the ruling classes. The Truths he spoke came as a thunderbolt from heaven.

He told them of their persecution of the holy men from Abel to Zacharias; and that God again had sent to them holy apostles, prophets, and seers; that the time was near when they would spurn them in the streets, would cast them into prison cells, and kill them with a fiend's delight.

He said to them: "Woe unto you, you Pharisees! you love the highest seats in synagogues and courts, and bid for salutations in the market place. Woe unto you, you tinseled gentry of the land! no man would ever think you servants of the Lord of hosts by what you do." "Woe unto you, you masters of the law! you snatch the keys of knowledge from the hands of men; you close the doors; you enter not yourselves, and suffer not the willing ones to enter in."

Jesus' words provoked the Pharisees, the lawyers, and scribes. They sought a legal way to shed his blood.

Later, after a silence with his disciples, Mary, his mother, and Miriam, who sang in the temple at Heliopolis, Jesus said: "Be on your guard; the leaven of the Pharisees is being thrown in every measure of the meal of life." He told them it was a poison that would blight the soul, and taint whatever it would touch; and said: "They do not seem to know that every thought and wish is photographed and then preserved within the Book of Life to be revealed at any time the masters will."

He said on to them: "You are not abandoned in your struggle for the crown of life; your Father lives, and you shall live." "God has a care for every living thing; the very petals of the rose he knows by name, and every one is numbered in his Book of Life; and every hair upon your head, and every drop of blood within your veins, he knows by number and by rhythm;" and "God will care for you who bear his image in your soul." "Fear not to make confession of the Christ before the sons of men, and God will own you as his own, as his sons and daughters, in the presence of the hosts of heaven."

Miriam stood forth and sang the song of victory; and, when the song was finished, Jesus revealed the symbolic character of the journey of Israel from Egypt to Canaan. He said: "Behold the way! The sons of men have groped for ages in the darkness of Egyptian night. The Pharaohs of sense have bound them with their chains. But God has whispered through the mists of time, and told them of a land of liberty and love. And he has sent his Logos forth to light the way. The Red Sea is the carnal mind. Behold, the Logos reaches out his hand; the sea divides; the carnal mind is reft in twain; the sons of men walk through dry shod. For just a little while men tread the wilderness of sin; the Logos leads the way; and when at last men stand upon the Jordan's brink, these waters stay, and men step forth into their own."

Then Jesus taught the multitudes to be good stewards of their wealth. He said: "Take heed, and covet not. The wealth of men does not consist in what they seem to have, in lands, in silver, and in gold. These things are only borrowed wealth. The wealth of soul lies in purity of life, and in the wisdom that descends from heaven."

He then took his disciples to Mary's home in Magdala. They dined together. Jesus called them "Little flock." He told them it was the Father's will that they should rule

the kingdom of the soul, that a ruler in the house of God
is servant to the Lord of hosts, and man serves God by
serving man. He taught them to be prepared to meet
their Lord; to be ever watchful lest he come and find them
unprepared.

After they had dined they went into a spacious hall in
Mary's home.

Lamaas, a priest of India, said to Jesus: "Pray tell us,
Lord, is this the dawn of Peace? Are you, indeed, the
Prince of Peace, that holy men have said would come?"

Jesus said: "Peace reigns today; it is the peace of death.
A stagnant pool abides in peace. When waters cease to
move they soon are laden with the seeds of death; corruption dwells in every drop. In life we find antagonists at
work. God sent me here to stir, unto its depths, the waters
of the sea of life. Peace follows strife; I come to slay this
peace of death. The prince of peace must first be prince ot
strife. The self and greed and doubt will rage into a fever
heat; and then, because of me, the earth will be baptized
in human blood. But right is king; and when the smoke
is cleared away the nations will learn to war no more; the
Prince of Peace will come to reign."

The Christines went to Bethsaida and taught. One
among the multitude arose, and told of a great disaster at
sea; that many were in distress, and asked what could be
done for them.

Jesus called for assistance from the men of Galilee, and
to Judas, one of the disciples, he said: "Bring forth our
treasure box; the money is not ours now; turn every farth-
ing to the help of those in such distress."

A lawyer said: "Rabboni, if God rules the worlds and
all that is in them, did he not bring about this storm?
Did he not slay these men? And was it done to punish
them for crimes?"

Jesus said: "We cannot look upon a single span of life
and judge of anything. There is a law that men must
recognize: Result depends on cause. Men are not motes to

float about within the air of one short life, and then be lost in nothingness. They are undying parts of the eternal whole that come and go, lo, many times into the air of earth and of the great beyond, just to unfold the God-like self. A cause may be a part of one brief life; results may not be noted till another life."

"If you would judge aright of human life, you must arise and stand upon the crest of time and note the thoughts and deeds of men as they have come up through the ages past; for we must know that man is not a creature made of clay to turn again to clay and disappear; he is a part of the eternal whole. There never was a time when he was not; a time will never come when he will not exist. And men are sick, and halt, and lame, and blind because they once transgressed the laws of perfect life; and every law of God must be fulfilled. If a wrong be done, the doer of the wrong must make it right; and when the wrongs have all been righted, then will man arise, and be at one with God."

In reference to the law of Cause and Effect, which the people of India call Karma, and the law of Reincarnation, we read in Flashlights of Truth a few quotations from the Chapter entitled: "Retributive Justice or Restoration."

"The first step for man, after he awakens to the fact concerning the law of Cause and Effect, is to endeavor to live so that he acts only toward his fellow-man as he 'would they would act toward him.' This is sowing good seed. Let man continue to thus live and do until he steps entirely away from the sowing and reaping condition."

"The law of Retributive Justice operates in unceasing power in carnality through the law of Cause and Effect." "Retributive Justice finally ends in Restoration. The man who has reached the peace of Restoration is freed from the law of Cause and Effect and has stepped aside from Birth and Death."

"When man has understanding complete, he will walk out from the law of Cause and Effect, and away from the wheel of Birth and Death, into the glorious liberty of the Sons of God."

Jesus taught beside the sea. He spoke in parables of the sower and the seed. Thomas, one of the disciples, asked Jesus why he taught thus in parable. Jesus said: "My words, like every Master's words, are dual in their sense. To you who know the language of the soul, my words have meanings far to deep for other men to comprehend. The other sense of what I say is all the multitude can understand; these words are food for them; the inner thoughts are food for you. Let every one reach forth, and take the food that he is ready to receive."

In the evening, in Philip's home, Peter said to Jesus: "Lord, will you explain to us the meaning of the parables you spoke to-day? The one about the wheat and tares especially?" Jesus said: "Gods kingdom is a duality; it has an outer and an inner form. The inner kingdom is the kingdom of the soul, the kingdom of the pure in heart. In the parable, the sower is the son of man; the field, the world; the good seed are the children of the light; the tares, the children of the dark, the enemy, the carnal self; the harvest day, the closing of an age; the reapers are the messengers of God." "Again, the kingdom of the soul is like a treasure hidden in a field which one has found, and straightway goes his way, and sells all that he has, and buys the field."

Then Jesus went alone into a mountain pass to pray.

A royal feast was held in Machaerus, east of the Bitter Sea in honor of the tetrarch. Herod, his wife Herodias, Salome, and all the men and women of the royal court were there.

After the feast was done, Salome, daughter of Herodias, danced before the king. Herod became entranced with her beauty and grace. He called her to his side and said: "Salome, you have won my heart, and you may ask and I will give you anything you wish." Salome told this to Herodias, and the mother said: "Go back, and say: 'Give me the head of John, the harbinger'.'' Salome told the ruler what she desired, and Herod granted her request.

The body of John was given unto holy men, who bore it to the Jordan where John first preached. They crossed the ford and carried it to Hebron through the Judean hills and laid it in the sacred ground where his parents lay.

Jesus and the foreign masters and the twelve crossed the sea of Galilee. A faithful friend of John said to Jesus: "Rabboni, let me follow where you go." Jesus said to him: "You seek a safe retreat from evil men; there is no safety for your life with me, for evil men will take my life as they have taken John's."

One evening while Jesus and the disciples were resting in a boat, a storm arose. Thomas called to Jesus, and Jesus stood; he raised his hand; he talked unto the spirits of the winds and waves as men would talk with men; and, lo, the winds blew not; the waves came tremblingly and kissed his feet; the sea was calm. Then Jesus said: "You men of faith, where is your faith? for you can speak, and winds and waves will hear and will obey." (Jesus, abiding in the consciousness of Aum, spoke Peace; and Peace was manifest.)

They went to Gadara and Jesus cleansed many who were obsessed with evil spirits. They then recrossed the sea and again were in Capernaum.

Matthew, one of the twelve, spread a sumptuous feast. Jesus, the foreign Masters, the disciples, and many others were guests. Nicodemus, a guest, asked Jesus if he could not harmonize his mighty work with that of the Pharisees and Scribes, and if the priesthood might not be a benefit to his divine philosophy? Jesus said to Nicodemus: "You can not put new wine in ancient skins, for when it purifies itself, lo, it expands; the ancient bottles can not bear the strain; they burst, and all the wine is lost. This Spirit-truth I bring is, to this generation, new; and if we put it in the ancient skins of Jewish forms, lo, it will all be lost. Behold the kingdom of the Christ! it is as old as God himself, and yet it is as new as the morning sun; it only can contain the truth of God."

While at the feast, Jairus, a ruler of the synagogue, asked Jesus if he would go, and speak the word, and save his only child. Jesus went out with Jairus; and, as they passed along the way, a woman, ill for many years, rose from her bed, and rushed out in the way of Jesus, saying: "If I can touch his garment, then I know I will be well." She touched him, and she was well. Jesus asked who touched his coat. The woman spoke and told him all. He said, to her: "Your faith has made you whole, go on your way in peace."

A servant of Jairus met them on their way, and said: "The child is dead." Jesus said: "Jairus, man of faith, do not permit your faith to waver in this trying hour. Lo, what is death? It is the passing of the soul out of the house of flesh. When man has risen up from doubt and fear, lo, he can cleanse the empty house and bring the tenant back again." He took Peter, James, and John, Jairus, and the mother of the child, and went into the chamber of the dead. He took the child by the hand and said: "Talitha cumi" (child, arise). The soul returned, and she arose.

To Nazareth the Christines journeyed with the foreign masters, Mary, and Miriam. On the Sabbath day Jesus went to the synagogue. He read from the book of Psalms and when he finished reading he spoke to the Pharisees, the priests, and scribes. He told them to reform, and turn to God that they might live. He said: "Let not your altars be accursed again with smoke of innocence; bring unto God a broken and contrite heart; lift from your fellowmen the burdens you have imposed."

They were all offended by the words he spoke.

Jesus said: "A prophet has no honor in his native land; he is not well received among his kin; his foes are in his home." He did not tarry long in Nazareth. The people had no faith in him; but as he went his way two blind men who had faith in Jesus asked him to open up their eyes. Jesus said: "Do you believe that I can open up your eyes and make you see?" They said: "Yea, Lord, we know that if you speak the word then we can see." Jesus touched their eyes and spoke the Word; he said: "According to your faith, so will it be." They opened up their eyes, and saw. And Jesus drove an unclean spirit out of one obsessed in Nazareth. The Pharisees were amazed; they said: "He heals the sick and casts the spirits out in Satan's name."

Jesus answered not, he and the others went their way to Cana. The Christines prayed in silence seven days. Then Jesus called his disciples, and said to them: "The people are bewildered; they need a shepherd's care; they wander here and there without a fold. The time is ripe, and you must go through all the towns of Galilee, and teach and heal."

He breathed upon the twelve, and said: "Receive the Holy Breath." He gave them the Word of power, and said: "By this omnific Word you shall cast spirits out: shall heal the sick, and bring the dead to life again. And, as you go, proclaim the kingdom of the Christ has come. You must go in faith, provide yourselves no crutch to lean upon. You go for me; you act for me. They who receive and welcome you, receive and welcome me; and they who shut their doors against your face, refuse to welcome me. Behold, I send you forth as sheep among a pack of wolves: and you must be as wise as serpents and as harmless as the doves. And when you meet a foe too great for you, behold, the son of man is at your door, and he can speak, and all the hosts of heaven will stand in your defense."

He said: "The Christ is king to-day, and men must recognize his power. He who loves not the Christ, which is the love of God, before all else, can never gain the prize of spirit consciousness. And they who love their parents or their children more than they love the Christ, can never wear the name of Christ."

Jesus then sent the twelve away by twos. They went

through all the towns of Galilee, and taught and healed in spirit and in power.

Jesus spent a time in prayer, then called the foreign masters, and said to them: "Behold, I sent the twelve apostles unto Israel, but you are sent to all the world. Our God is God of every child of India, of Persia, of Greece and Rome, of Egypt, and of the mighty lands across the seas. Go on your way, and as you go proclaim the gospel of the Christ." He breathed upon them, and said: "Receive the Holy Breath." He gave to each the Word of power. He sent them forth, and every land was blessed. Then Jesus went across the hills of Galilee. He reached the coast of Tyre, and abode in the home of Rachel many days. Then he dwelt a time in Sidon by the sea.

He journeyed on. In the Lebanon hills and valleys he walked. His mission upon earth was drawing to a close and he sought for strength. Upon Mount Hermon's lofty peaks he stood and talked with God. Masters of olden times revealed themselves, and they talked long about the kingdom of the Christ; and of the mighty works that had been done; about the coming conquest of the cross; about the victory over death.

Then Jesus journeyed to Cæsarea Philippi, and tarried in Susanna's home. He went through all Decapolis and to Gadara, to prepare his friends for the day of Calvary; and then he went aboard a ship, and crossed the sea.

The people welcomed Jesus in Capernaum, and soon the twelve returned, and told him of their journey over Galilee. The Master heard and when they had finished, he said: "Well done." (Aquarian Gospel, 108: 123 in part.)

THE MINISTRY AND TEACHING OF JESUS, *Continued*

JESUS' TRANSFIGURATION

THE twelve disciples had reached the state of spirit consciousness where Jesus could reveal to them the deeper meaning of his mission to the world.

He said to them: "The time is short, and I have many things to say to you." He took them to a desert place to rest awhile near Julius Bethsaida.

Multitudes followed them, and in compassion Jesus taught them through the day. When evening came, Jesus fed the multitude. Five thousand sat in groups of twelve and Jesus took five barley loaves and two small fish and looking up to heaven he spoke the sacred Word. And then he broke the bread, and gave it to the twelve, and gave the fish unto the twelve, and said: "Go to and feed the multitudes."

The people were bewildered by this act of power, and said: "All Hail the King!"

Then Jesus went alone to pray.

The twelve took boat to reach Capernaum. A storm arose and they were filled with fear; but in the blinding storm they saw a form move on the waves. John discerned the form, and said: "It is the Lord."

Peter said: "My Lord! If this be truly you, bid me to come to you upon the waves." The form reached forth his arms, and said: "Come on." Peter stepped upon the waves, and walked until he thought: "What if these waves should break beneath my feet?" The waves did break, and he began to sink. He cried: "O save me, Lord.

or I am lost." Jesus took his hand, and said: "O you of
little faith! why did you doubt?"

(As Peter's faith was tried, so all who follow in the
path are tried. Faith is a gift from God and is bestowed
upon man in answer to his prayer. It can not be manufactured by the mind. St. Paul said: "Faith is the substance of things hoped for and the evidence of things not
seen." Man's faith is strengthened with every victory over
obstacles that confront him in the path. Faith merges into
understanding, then into knowing, and finally into realization. Jesus did not require faith. He knew God.)

When the storm had ceased, Jesus and the twelve were
near the shore. In the valley of Gennesaret Jesus taught.
Later, Jesus went to Capernaum with the twelve, and
taught in the synagogue. His disciples were aggrieved, and
many followers turned away when Jesus said: "I came in
flesh to do the will of God, and, lo, this flesh and blood
are filled with Christ; and so I am the living bread that
comes from heaven. And when you eat this flesh and
drink this blood you will have everlasting life; and, if you
will, you may become the bread of life. The Christ is
everlasting life; he came from heaven; he has the keys of
heaven, and no man enters into heaven except he fills himself with Christ."

They could not comprehend the parable, and Jesus said:
"You stumble and you fall before the truth; what will
you do when you shall see this flesh and blood transmuted
into higher form? What will you say when you see the
son of man ascending on the clouds of heaven? What
will you say when you shall see the son of man sit on the
throne of God?"

Then Jesus took the twelve across the sea to Decapolis
that he might reveal to them the things that were to come.
They spent three days in prayer, and Jesus said: "Behold
the time is near when I will walk with you in flesh no
more. Lo, I am come as pattern for the sons of men, and
I have not refrained from helpfulness. When I passed the
seven tests in Heliopolis, I consecrated life and all I had, to

save the world. God gave to me the saving Word, and I
have spoken it, and healed the sick, drove unclean spirits
out, and raised the dead. And I have shown you how to
speak the Word; and I have given you the Word. In just a
little while we turn our faces toward Jerusalem and one
of you who hear me now will betray me into wicked
hands. The Scribes and Pharisees will bring false charges
up, and hale me into court; and, by consent of Rome, I
will be crucified."

Peter said: "My Lord, this shall not be." Jesus answered: "A savior of the world can not resist. But my
example will not end with death. My body will be laid
within a tomb. And then, symbolic of the ascent of the
soul to higher life, my flesh within the tomb will disappear; will be transmuted into higher form, and in the
presence of you all I will ascend to God."

The Christines then went to Dalmanatha by the sea.
Jesus told the twelve about the inner light that can not
fail; about the kingdom of the Christ within the soul;
about the power of faith; about the secret of the resurrection of the dead; about immortal life; and how the living
may go forth and help the dead.

Then they journeyed to Cæsarea Philippi. The master
said as they walked together: "What do the people say
about the son of man? Who do they think I am?" The
disciples said: "Some say you are David come again; some
say that you are Enoch, Solomon, or Seth. The foreign
masters say that you are Gautama come again; some say
Melchizedek, the king of peace."

And Jesus asked: "Who do you think I am?" Peter
said: "You are the Christ, the love of God made manifest to men."

Peter was chosen as apostolic leader. Jesus said: "Your
confession is the corner-stone of faith, a rock of strength;
and on this rock the church of Christ is built. Against it
all the powers of hades and of death can not prevail. Behold, I give to you the keys to open up the doors of safety
for the sons of men. The Holy Breath will come upon

you and the ten, and in Jerusalem you shall stand before
the nations of the earth, and there proclaim the covenant
of God with men."

Then Jesus and the twelve went to Susanna's home as
guests.

Many people came, and Jesus said to them: "Behold,
you come to see, but that means naught. If you would
have the benedictions of the Christ, take up your cross,
and follow me. If you would find the spirit life, the life
of man in God, then you must walk a narrow way and
enter through a narrow gate. The way is Christ, the
gate is Christ, and you must come up by the way of Christ.
No man comes unto God but by the Christ."

Then Jesus, Peter, James, and John went to the mountain top to pray. As Jesus prayed a brilliant light appeared; his form became as radiant as a precious stone; his
face shone like the sun; his garments seemed as white as
snow; the son of man became the Son of God. He was
transfigured that the men of earth might see the possibilities of man.

Moses and Elijah appeared, and talked with Jesus about
the coming trial of the Lord; about his death; his rest
within the tomb; about the wonders of the resurrection
morn; the transmutation of his flesh and his ascension on
the clouds of light; all symbolic of the path that every
man must tread to become a son of God.

Then from out the glory of the upper world a voice
was heard that said: "This is the son of man, my chosen
one to manifest the Christ to men. Let all the earth hear
him."

Soon the Master and the twelve returned to Capernaum.

Jesus heard his disciples dispute among themselves.
They were questioning among themselves who was the
greatest in the sight of God. Jesus said: "For shame! the
greatest is the servant of the rest." He called to a little
child, and took it in his arms, and said: "The greatest
is the little child, and if you would be great at all you
must become as is this child in innocence, in truth, in

purity in life. Great men scorn not the little things of
earth. If you would enter in the kingdom gate, you must
be as humble as this little child."

Among the multitudes that followed Jesus were many
who were not Jews. Jesus called seventy of these and sent
them forth in twos to every nation. He said to them: "Go
in the sacred name; trust God, and you will never come to
want; and let your salutation be: 'Peace be to all; good
will to all.' "

Then Jesus went to Jerusalem through Samaria. As he
went through Sychar, ten lepers saw him and asked him
to speak the word that they might be made clean. Jesus
said to them: "Go forth and show yourselves unto the
priests." They went, and their leprosy was healed. Just
one returned to thank the master and praise the Lord.
Jesus said: "You have revealed your heart, and shown
that you are worthy of the power; behold, the nine will
find again their leprous hands and feet."

Jesus taught in the temple; he said: "Whoever is
athirst may come to me and drink. He who believes in me
and in the Christ whom God has sent, may drink the cup
of life, and from his inner parts shall streams of living
waters flow. The Holy Breath will overshadow him, and
he will breathe the Breath, and speak the words, and live
the life."

The rulers were enraged by his words. The Pharisees
and Scribes still sought to find a cause whereby they might
condemn him by his words.

When the feast was done Jesus with Peter, James, and
John sat in the temple treasury. The people thronged the
temple courts, and Jesus said to them: "I am the lamp;
Christ is the oil of life; the Holy Breath is fire. Behold
the light! and he who follows me shall not walk in the
dark, but he shall have the light of life. My works bear
witness to the truth I speak. As man I could not speak
these words, they are the words of Holy Breath; and my
Father testifies for me."

A lawyer said: "Where does your father live?" Jesus said to him: "You know me not or you would know my Father; and if you knew the Father you would know the son, because the Father and the son are one." "I come to manifest the Christ to men and you receive me not, and you will dwell in darkness and in the shadow of the grave till you believe the words I speak."

To the people who believed in him he said: "If you abide in Christ, and Christ abide in you, and if you keep my words within your heart, you are the way, you are the disciples in the way, and you shall know what is the truth; and truth shall make you free."

To a lawyer Jesus said: "Your father Abraham rejoiced to see my day; he saw it, and was glad." The lawyer said: "You simple man, you are not fifty years of age; have you seen Abraham?" Jesus said: "Before Abraham was I am." The lawyer could not understand. (Jesus was conscious that he was a son of God; he spoke in the consciousness of the Atman self, the Divinity within his temple, who came forth from the Father, Aum, glorified in His own image and likeness before the world was.)

Jesus, Peter, James, and John went to Bethany to the home of Lazarus and there he taught. Martha was busy with her guests, but Mary sat at Jesus' feet to hear him speak the words of life. Jesus said to Martha: "You grow a-weary by your care for little things, and slight the one thing needed most of all. Your sister here has chosen far the better part, a part that none can take away."

In the evening, Jesus, Lazarus, and the disciples went out beyond the village to pray. Lazarus said to Jesus: "Teach me to pray." Jesus gave him the model prayer, and said to him: "The answer to your prayer may not appear in fullness in a little time. Be not discouraged, pray again, and then again, for God will hear."

In Jerusalem Jesus healed a man blind from birth. Peter said: "Lord, if disease and imperfections all are caused by sin, who was the sinner in this case, the parents or the man himself?" Jesus said: "Affliction is a certain sign that one has debts to pay. Behold this man! Once in another life he was a cruel man, and in a cruel way destroyed the eyes of one, a fellow man. The parents of this man once turned their faces on a blind and helpless man, and drove him from their door."

When the Pharisees heard the story of the man who had been blind, and heard him say, that nothing but the power of God could do such things as Jesus did, they cast him from the synagogue.

Jesus found the man, and said to him: "Do you believe in God and in the son of God?" He said: "I do believe in God; but who is he, the son of God, of whom you speak?" Jesus said: "The son of God is he who speaks to you," and added: "All men are sons of God by birth; God is the father of the race; but all are not the sons of God by faith." "He who believes, and does the will of God, is son of God by faith."

In joy the man exclaimed: "Lord, I believe in God and in the son of God."

The people pressed about, and Jesus told them of the sheepfold and of the shepherd, and then said: "The shepherd calls his sheep by name; they hear his call, and follow him through the gate into the fold." He said: "Christ is the gateway of the fold; I am the shepherd of the sheep, and he who follows me through Christ shall come into the fold where living waters flow, and where rich pastures are. I am the shepherd of the sheep; I know the sheep of God; they know my voice, as God knows me and I know him. The Father loves me with a deathless love, because I lay my life down for the sheep. I lay my life down when I will, but I may take it up again; for every son of God by faith has power to lay his mortal flesh aside and take it up again. These words I have received from God." (Aquarian Gospel, 124; 139 in part.)

Then Jesus left Jerusalem and tarried with Massalian certain days.

*   *   *   *

Within each mortal is the Divine-man; he who "never was born and never will die"—the image and likeness of God, Atman—the son of God. (From Flashlights of Truth.)

There is a river that spans the gulf between the third dimension (man's carnal mind) and the fourth dimension (the kingdom, Aum). This is the river of Love, the Christ. All men must follow Jesus through Christ to enter into the fold. When this is accomplished by the Father's help, Atman, God's image, expresses. And Jesus says: "Lo, I am with you all the way."

JESUS' CHRISTINE MINISTRY, *Continued*

JESUS, Peter, James, and John began their journey back to Galilee. They went through Samaria and the people thronged the ways to see the one, whom the seventy had told about. Jesus healed the sick, and taught.

Again they reached Capernaum. The seventy were there, and they told Jesus of the works they did in the sacred name. And they rejoiced.

Jesus said: "As you went I heard a Master say: 'Well done'; but you may not rejoice because you have the power to heal the sick and make the devils tremble by the Word; for such rejoicing is from Carnal self; you may rejoice because the nations of the earth have ears to hear the Word, and eyes to see the glory of the Lord, and hearts to feel the inner breathing of the Holy Breath."

Jesus said again: "Lo, I have gone before you many moons, and I have given to you the bread of heaven and the cup of life; have been your buckler and your stay; but now that you have learned the way, and have the strength to stand alone, behold, I lay my body down and go to Him, the All. In forty days we will turn our faces toward Jerusalem where I will find the altar of the Lord, and give my life in willing sacrifice for men."

They arose, and went into every town and village on the coast; and Jesus healed, and taught.

One of Jesus' followers asked of him: "Lord, are there few that enter into life?" Jesus said: "The way is rough that leads to life, the gate is narrow and is guarded well; but every one who seeks in faith shall find the way, and they who know the word may enter in. But many seek

the way for selfish gain; they pound upon the gate of
life; but it is fast. Behold, I say, the last shall be the
first, the first shall be the last. All men are called unto the
kingdom of the Christ; but few are chosen, for the pure in
heart alone can see the king."

As Jesus spoke a Pharisee came up and told him that,
if he would save his life, he must flee instantly; that offi-
cers were seeking him, and Herod would have him slain.
Jesus said: "Why is it that the Pharisees are so con-
cerned about my life?" He said: "Go say to him, I need
not fear in Galilee, for I must meet the cruel wrath of men
in Jerusalem."

And Jesus told the people of the difficulties of the path
of discipleship. Many were following him for selfish gain.
He said to them: "If you would follow me in love, and
be disciples of the Holy Breath and gain at last the crown
of life, you must leave all there is of carnal life behind.
Be not deceived; stay men, and count the cost. If one
would build a tower, or a home, he first sits down and
counts the cost to be assured that he has gold enough to
finish it; for well he knows that if he makes a failure of
his enterprise he may lose all his wealth, and be the butt
of ridicule. Count well the cost before you start to follow
me; it means the giving up of life, and all you have. If
you love father, mother, wife, or child, more than you love
the Christ, you can not follow me. If you love wealth or
honor more than you love the Christ, you can not follow
me. The paths of carnal life do not run up the mountain
side toward the top, they run around the mount of life;
and if you go straight to the upper gate of consciousness
you cross the path of carnal life. And this is how men
bear the cross."

And then he said: "Take up the cross, and follow me
through Christ into the path of true discipleship; this is
the path that leads to life. This way of life is called the
pearl of greatest price, and he who finds it must put all he
has beneath his feet."

One day as the Lord was standing by the sea, one asked him if God bestowed rewards as man bestows rewards for what is done. Jesus answered: "Men never know what other men have done; this life is such a seeming life. One man may seem to do a mighty work, and be adjudged by men as worthy of a great reward. Another man may seem to be a failure in the harvest fields of life, and be dishonored in the face of men. Men do not know the hearts of men; God only knows their hearts, and when the day is done he may reward with life the man who fell beneath the burdens of the day, and turn away the man who was the idol of the hearts of men."

In Tiberius, Jesus taught the twelve many things on the inner life; and when the multitudes came, he told them the parable of the prodigal son, who had squandered all his father's wealth and when nothing else remained he found employment in the fields to care for swine. But after many days he found himself; he said: "I will arise, and go to my Father's house." And he arose, and sought his Father's house, and while yet a long way off his mother saw him coming. The Father came, and together they walked a-down the way to meet their son, and there was great joy in the mother's and in the father's heart.

In Flashlights of Truth, we read: "Let the awakened man with his reason follow this parable of Jesus, and perceive that he himself is the prodigal son; because all men were in Paradise (at home in the Father's house) and all men passed out from that concept into the Garden of Eden, then out into the world, where man became lost in the maze of illusive shadows which form and compose carnality." "Jesus in teaching the man who is awake to the reality of his individuality, endeavors to show him that he will ever find that the carnal life has not the element of permanency, neither enduring happiness, and that contentment, which is the companion of Divine Satisfaction, is not to be found within its domain, but ever dwells just behind the curtain of carnality."

Jesus' work in Galilee was finished. Many came from

afar to receive his benediction. Miriam sang the song of
victory, and Jesus prayed that love and mercy might rest
upon them all. He said: "The lamp is taken from their
midst, and if the inner light be not aflame, lo, they must
tread the ways of darkness and of death." He said farewell, and went with his mother, the twelve, and others
to Jerusalem.

In the temple at Jerusalem, Jesus was approached by a
scribe who asked if he would not tell the people if he was
the Messiah, that their prophets had said would come.
Jesus said: "Lo, I have told you many times, but you
believed it not. No man can do the work that I have done,
and bring to men the truth as I have brought the truth,
who did not come from God. What I have done and said
are witnesses for me. You can not hear the voice of God
because your ears are closed, and your hearts are full of
self."

Jesus rebuked the Jews for treachery, and they attempt-
ed to stone him. Joseph, member of the great Sanhedrim
of the Jews, appealed to their reason, and they refrained
from violence. Jesus said: "Lo, I have healed your sick,
have caused your blind to see, your deaf to hear, your lame
to walk, and cast out unclean spirits from your friends;
for which of these great works would you desire to take
my life?" The Jews replied: "You are but man, and still
you say that you are God," and he replied: "If you believe not what I say, you must have faith in what I do;
and you should see the Father in these works, and know
that I dwell in the Father-God, and that the Father dwells
in me." He withdrew himself from sight, and went with
the twelve to Jericho.

Word came from Bethany that Lazarus, his friend, was
very ill; but Jesus did not hasten to him, as he was implored to do. He spent two days in Araba and then went
on to Bethany. Ruth and Martha met him at the village
gate. Martha said to Jesus: "You are too late, for Lazarus is dead." Jesus said: "Behold, for Lazarus shall live
again;" and bade them return and tell their sister and his

mother and the prophetess to meet him at the gate. When they met, Mary said: "Why did you tarry thus? If you had been with us our brother dear would not have died."

Jesus went to the home of Lazarus and said: "Where is the tomb in which he lies?" And Jesus wept. They rolled away the stone and Jesus lifted up his eyes to heaven and said: "My Father-God, thou who hast ever heard my prayers; I thank thee now; and that these multitudes may know that thou hast sent me forth, that I am thine and thou art mine, make strong the Word of power." He spoke the Word, and said: "O Lazarus, awake!" Lazarus arose and came forth from the tomb. The people were amazed and multitudes confessed their faith in Jesus.

When the Pharisees heard about the resurrection of the dead, they met in council and sought a plan by which they might put Jesus to death. They feared that, through the Romans, Jesus might take the throne and they would lose their place and power.

Caiaphas was the high priest and each day the Jews conferred with him, maturing plans to put the Lord to death.

The feast of spring was at hand, and all loyal Jews were going to Jerusalem. The priests and Pharisees were all alert; they said: "This Jesus will be at the feast, and we must not permit that he shall slip away again." They commanded every man to help to apprehend the Lord.

As Jesus drew near Jerusalem he paused, and wept over the holy city of the Jews. He said: "Jerusalem, Jerusalem, the holy city of the Jews! yours was the glory of the Lord; but you have cast the Lord away. Your eyes are closed, you can not see the king; the kingdom of the Lord of heaven and earth has come; you comprehend it not."

Great excitement reigned as Jesus entered Jerusalem. He went directly to the temple. It was filled with people pressing hard to see the king. The temple courts were filled with children praising God. Jesus taught and healed the sick on the Sabbath day.

During the first part of the week he taught in the temple. He admonished the people to walk in the light. To the Priests, Scribes, and Pharisees, Jesus said: "The Lord of heaven and earth has spread a sumptuous feast, and you were bidden first of all; but you have found the door into the banquet hall so low that you must bow your heads and fall down on your knees to enter in; you have scorned the king who made the feast; refused to bow your heads, and fall down on your knees; and you have gone your way. John came to you in righteousness; he brought the truth, but you believed him not. I tell you now, as I have told you many times, the many have been called, but chosen are the few."

He rebuked the Pharisees and Scribes for their hypocrisy. He pronounced many woes upon them, and as he looked about he said: "Jerusalem, Jerusalem, thou cruel city of Jerusalem, that slays the prophets in the streets and kills the holy men whom God has sent to you! Lo, I would oft have gathered you as children to the fold of God; but you would not. You have rejected God, and now your house is desolate, and you shall see me not again till you can say, Thrice blessed is the son of man who comes as son of God."

The disciples were standing by, and Jesus said: "The hour has come; the son of man is ready to be glorified, and it can not be otherwise. Except a grain of wheat fall into earth and die it can be nothing but a grain of wheat; but if it die it lives again, and from its grave a hundred grains of wheat arise."

He prayed for strength to bear the burdens, whatever they were, and said: "This is the hour for which I came to earth; O Father, glorify thy name!" The place was filled with a brilliant light; the people were afraid. A voice that seemed to come from heaven said: "I have both glorified my name and yours, and I will honor them again."

The people said an angel spoke, and Jesus said to them: "This voice was not for me; it was for you, that you

might know that I am come from God." He stood upon
the temple porch, and made his last appeal to the multitude; and then he said: "Jerusalem, with all your glory
and your crimes, Farewell."

He went with his disciples to Mount Olive, and prophe-
sied the destruction of Jerusalem, and told of the disasters
that would mark the conclusion of the age. He said: "Before these days shall come, behold, false Christs and poor
deluded prophets will arise in many lands, and they will
show forth signs, and do a multitude of mighty works;
and they will lead astray the many who are not wise; and
many of the wise will be deceived. And now I tell you
once again, when men shall say: 'The Christ is in the
wilderness,' go you not forth. And if they say: 'The
Christ is in the secret place,' believe it not; for when he
comes the world will know that he has come; for as the
morning light comes from the east and shines unto the
west, so shall the son of man come down upon the clouds
of heaven in power."

He told them to take heed, to watch and pray, that they
might meet the Lord in joy and not in grief; for no man
knew the hour when the son of man would come; and
before the day would come the Father-God would send
his messengers abroad to all the corners of the earth to
proclaim that the Prince of Peace would come.

Then Jesus and his disciples went back to Bethany.

On Wednesday of the week, they went to Olive to
pray. After seven hours of prayer Jesus called the disciples
close, and said: "This day the curtain parts, and we will
step beyond the veil into the secret courts of God." He
opened up the meaning of the hidden way and of the
Holy Breath, and told them of the Book of Life where
all the thoughts and words of men are written down.
And Jesus said: "These things may not be spoken out
aloud; they never may be written down; they are the
messages of Silenceland; they are the Breathings of the
inner heart of God;" and then he gave them lessons to
teach to other men. He said: "Teach them to pray and

to be prepared at every moment of the day; for, when they least expect, the Lord will come." He gave them the parable of the ten virgins; five of whom were wise and had their lamps filled with oil; the other five, the foolish virgins, had no oil to burn. When the bridegroom came the five with lamps burning went forth to meet the groom.

Again he said: "Be ready every moment of the day and night; Behold, when he will come with all his messengers of light, the Book of Life shall be opened up, and everyone can read the records he has written for himself; and according to their records men will find their own."

And in the sifting time, to those who are prepared the judge will say: "You served the sons of men and whatsoever you have done for them you have done for me." To the others he will say: "Your life was full of self; you served the self and not your fellowman, and when you slighted one of these you slighted and neglected me." He said: "Those who have ears to hear and hearts to understand will comprehend these parables." And then he said: "In two days the great passover feast will come; and, lo, the son of man will be betrayed into the hands of wicked men. He will give his life upon the cross, and men will know that he, the son of man, is Son of God."

In honor of the Nazarine Master, Bar-Simon gave a feast in Bethany. He had been a leper, but was cleansed by Jesus by the sacred word. Lazarus was a guest, and his sisters Ruth and Martha served.

Mary took costly perfume and poured it upon Jesus' head and feet, and Judas censured her extravagance.

Jesus said: "Mary knows the sadness of the coming days; she has anointed me beforehand for my burial; the gospel of the Christ will everywhere be preached, and he who tells the story of the Christ will tell about this day; and what was done by Mary at this hour will be a sweet memorial to her wherever men abide."

After the feast Jesus went to Lazarus' home.

The priests and Pharisees in Jerusalem were making plans to seize him. It was Ananias' plan to find Jesus with his disciples while at prayer; and their secret place was to be revealed by Judas, one of the twelve. Caiaphas, the high priest agreed.

Judas reasoned that it might be well for Jesus to tell the priests about his claims when alone; and if they were intent to do him harm, Jesus had the power to disappear, and go his way. He told Ananias that he would lead the way and make known by a kiss which one was the Lord.

On Thursday Jesus said to his disciples: "This is God's Remembrance day, and we will eat the Paschal supper all alone." He sent Peter, James, and John to Jerusalem to prepare the Pasch; and bade them go to Nicodemus, a ruler of the Jews, and say to him: "The Lord would have you set apart your banquet hall where he may eat his last passover with the twelve."

When the hour came to eat the feast, the disciples were each anxious for an honored seat. Jesus said to them: "My friends, would you contend for self just as the shadows of this night of gloom comes on?" He arose, took a basin of water, and washed each disciple's feet. This was the lesson of the hour. Jesus said: "You call me Master; such I am. If then your Lord and Master kneel and wash your feet, should you not wash each other's feet, and thus show forth your willingness to serve?" And then he said: "This is an hour when I can truly praise the name of God, for I have greatly wished to eat with you this feast before I pass the veil; for I will eat it not again until anew I eat it with you in the kingdom of our Father-God."

They sang the Hebrew Song, and ate the Pasch; and as they ate Jesus said: "Behold, for one of you will turn away this night, and will betray me into wicked hands." The disciples were amazed. John touched the Master, and said: "Which one of us is so depraved as to betray his Lord?" Judas said: "Is it I, Lord?" Jesus said: "He is the one who now has put his hand with mine into the dish." It was the hand of Judas, and he arose and went away.

Jesus sat in silent thought; then took a loaf of bread that had not been broken, and said: "This loaf is symbol of my body, and bread is the symbol of the bread of life; as I break this loaf, so shall my flesh be broken as a pattern for the sons of men; as you eat this bread, so shall you eat the bread of life." He gave each a piece of bread to eat.

Then he took a cup of wine, and said: "Blood is the life; this is the life-blood of the grape; it is the symbol of the life of him who gives his life for men; as you drink this wine, if you drink in faith, you drink the life of Christ." He supped, and passed the cup, and the disciples supped. He said: "This is the feast of life, the great passover of the son of man, the supper of the Lord; and you shall often eat the bread and drink the wine. And when you eat this bread and drink this wine remember me." (Aquarian Gospel, 140; 160 in part.)

This sacred communion with the Lord has been observed by all who follow in his path, in remembrance of Him.

The sacred bread and wine through prayer is raised by the Father to the vibration of the Love Essence of Aum, to which Jesus' body was raised through his ascension unto God; so all who partake of it in faith and love, partake of this Divine Essence, the Body of the Lord.

LESSON XI.

PART ONE

EVENTS LEADING TO THE CRUCIFIXION OF JESUS

THE CRUCIFIXION

JUDAS went out to betray his Lord. Jesus said to the eleven: "The hour has come; the son of man will now be glorified. I give to you a new command: 'As I love you and give my life for you, so you shall love the world, and give your life to save the world. Love one another as you love yourselves, and then the world will know that you are sons of God, disciples of the son of man whom God has glorified.' "

He looked upon the eleven, and said: "You all will be estranged from me this night. The prophet said, 'He will smite the shepherd of the sheep; the sheep will flee and hide away; but after I am risen from the dead, lo, you will come again, and I will go before you into Galilee.' "

Peter said: "My Lord, though every other man forsake you I will not."

Jesus answered: "O Simon Peter, lo, your zeal is greater than your fortitude! Behold, for Satan cometh up to sift you as a pan of wheat, but I have prayed that in your faith you shall not fail; that after trial you may stand a tower of strength. I go unto my Fatherland and will prepare a place for you that where I am there you may be."

He said: "I am the way, the truth, and the life; I manifest the Christ of God. No man can reach my Fatherland except he comes with me through Christ. If you had

96

known and comprehended me, then you would know my Father-God. He who has seen the son has seen the Father, for in the son the Father has revealed himself."

Jesus encouraged the faithful men saying: "He who believes in me and in my Father-God shall say and do what I have said and done; yea, more, he shall do greater works than I have ever done, because I go to him whose works we do, and then I can reach forth my hand in helpfulness." "And now I go my way; but I will pray my Father-God and he will send another comforter to you, who will abide with you. Behold, this Comforter of God, the Holy Breath, is one with God, but she is one the world can not receive because it sees her not; it knows her not. I will not leave you desolate; but in the Christ, which is the love of God made manifest to men, I will be with you all the way."

The disciples of Jesus were deeply grieved. He said to them: "Grieve not because I go away, for it is best that I should go away; if I go not, the Comforter will not come to you." And Jesus added: "There are a multitude of things yet to be said; things that this age can not receive, because it can not comprehend. But, lo, I say, before the great day of the Lord shall come, the Holy Breath will make all mysteries known—the mysteries of the soul, of life, of death, of immortality; the oneness of a man with every other man and with his God. Then will the world be led to Truth, and man will be the truth."

Jesus prayed for his disciples and for all who would believe on him and accept the Christ. He lifted his eyes to heaven, and said: "My Father-God, the hour has come; the son of man must now be lifted from the earth, and may he falter not, that all the world may know the power of sacrifice; for as I give my life for men, lo, men must give their lives for other men. I came to do thy will, O God; and in the sacred name, the Christ is glorified, that men may see the Christ as life, as light, as love, as truth; and through the Christ become themselves the life, the light, the love, the truth."

Then together they sang the Jewish Song of praise.

As Jesus and the eleven went out a Roman guard approached, and said: "All hail! Is one of you the man from Galilee? I seek for Jesus, who is called the Christ."

Jesus answered: "Here am I."

The guard said: "I bear a message from the governor. He would confer with you."

Jesus bade his disciples await him at the Kidron, and went with the guard to Pilate. The governor met him at the gate, and said: "Young man, I have a word to say that may be well for you. I have observed your works and words three years and more; I have often stood in your defense when your own countrymen would fain have stoned you as a criminal; but now the Priests and Scribes and Pharisees have stirred the common people to a stage of frenzied wantonness and cruelty and they intend to take your life. There is no safety for you but in flight. wait not until the morning sun."

Jesus said: "The coward flees when danger comes; but he who comes to seek and save the lost must give his life in willing sacrifice for those he comes to seek and save. Before the Pasch has been consumed, lo, all this nation will be cursed by shedding blood of innocence; and even now the murderers are at the door."

Pilate said: "It shall not be; the sword of Rome will be unsheathed to save your life."

Jesus said: "Nay, Pilate, nay; there are no armies large enough in all the world to save my life." He bade Pilate farewell, and disappeared.

Soon Jesus met his disciples at the brook of Kidron.

Massalian, a friend of Jesus, lived near the brook. In the orchard was a sacred knoll he called Gethsemane. Jesus bade eight disciples to tarry by the brook. He took Peter, James, and John to Gethsemane to pray. They sat beneath an olive tree, and Jesus opened up the mysteries of life to them. He said: "The spirit of Eternity is One unmanifest; and this is God the Father, God the Mother, God the Son in One. In life of manifests the One became the Three, God the Father is the power of heaven and earth; God, the Mother is the Holy Breath; God the Son, is Christ; Christ is Love. I came to manifest this love to men."

He told them that he had been subject to the trials and temptations of the human race; that he had overcome the flesh with all its passions and appetites; and that what he did all men could do. He said: "I am now about to demonstrate the power of man to conquer death; for every man is God made flesh. I will lay down my life, and I will take it up again, that you may know the mysteries of life, of death, and of the resurrection of the dead. I lay me down in flesh; but I will rise in spirit form with power to manifest myself so mortal eyes can see. In a trinity of days I will show forth the all of life, the all of death, the meaning of the resurrection of the dead. And you, my three, who constitute the inner circle of the church of Christ, will show to men the attributes of God."

Then Jesus left the three to watch with him and went alone to talk to God. He prayed long; his soul was firm but the human flesh shrank back. In agony he prayed; his brow was bathed in blood. He went to the disciples, and found them all asleep, while he was wrestling with the greatest foe of men. He awakened them, and said: "Could you not watch with me a single hour?" He went again, and prayed: "O God, I yield to thee; thy will be done."

They went to the Kidron, and as Jesus talked with the eleven they saw a band approaching, and Judas led the way.

Jesus went alone to meet the men; he said: "Why are you here, you men? Whom do you seek?" They said: "We seek the man from Galilee, Jesus, who calls himself the Christ." Jesus answered: "Here am I." He raised his hands and a great light filled the orchard; the men shrank back; many of them fled.

Judas stood beside Ananias; then, coming to the Lord, he said: "My Lord," and then he kissed him as a sign that he was Jesus.

The mob laid hold of Jesus and were binding him with chains. He said: "What are these chains but links of reeds." He raised his hands; the chains were broken, and they fell to earth. Malchus, servant of Caiaphas would have smitten Jesus, but Peter smote Malchus with his sword.

Jesus said: "Stay, Peter, stay; put up your sword; you are not called to fight with swords and clubs. I do not need protection by the sons of men; for I could call, this moment, and a legion, yea, twelve legions of the messengers of God, would come and stand in my defense; but then it is not well."

Jesus laid his hand on Malchus' wound, and it was healed.

The mob then rushed upon the eleven, and each one fled to save his life. Later, John and Peter followed behind the mob and went into Jerusalem.

Jesus was taken to the palace hall of Caiaphas, the high priest of the Jews.

The galleries were filled with Scribes and Pharisees sworn as witnesses against the Lord.

Jesus was charged as an imposter and a foe, a profaner of the holy days, a blasphemer who said that he was a Son of God, and that he and God were one; and many other charges.

A hundred men who had been bribed testified and swore that the charges all were true, and Jesus said no word.

They bound Jesus, and took him to the great Sanhedrim of the Jews. The witnesses testified before the council of the Jews. The lawyers weighed the evidence. Nicodemus pleaded for justice, and when the witnesses were brought before the judges no two agreed. In face of all the evidence, the council feared to sentence Jesus.

Caiaphas said: "You man from Galilee, before the living God, I now command that you shall answer me. Are you the Christ, the son of God?"

Jesus said: "If I would answer 'Yes,' you would not hear nor yet believe. If I would answer 'No,' I would be like your witnesses, and stand a liar in the sight of man and God. But this I say: "The time will come when you will see the son of man upon the throne of power and coming in the clouds of heaven."

Caiaphas said to the people: "Have you not heard enough? What shall we do with him?"

The people said: "Put him to death." Jesus, the man from Galilee, resisted not. He was taken to the palace of Pilate, the Roman Governor, for his confirmation of the sentence of the court.

The Jews gave Pilate their bill of charges and their evidence; and, as Jesus stood before him, Pilate read to him the charges of the Jews. And Pilate said: "What is your answer to this bill? Are these charges true or false?"

Jesus said: "Why should I plead before an earthly court? The charges have been verified by perjured men; what need I say? Yes, I am king; but carnal man can not behold the king, nor see the kingdom of God; it is within. If I had been a king as carnal man is king, my servants would have stood in my defense, and I would not have willingly surrendered to the minions of the Jewish law. I have no testimony from the sons of men. God is my witness, and my words and deeds bear witness to the truth. And every man who comprehends the truth will hearken to my words, and in his soul give witness unto me."

Pilate asked: "What is the truth?"

Jesus answered: "Truth is the God who knows. It is the changeless one. The Holy Breath is truth; she changes not, and can not pass away."

Pilate could not find Jesus guilty of a crime; and, since Jesus was a man from Galilee, he sent him to Herod, the governor of Galilee, who was in Jerusalem, that he might be the judge.

To Herod's questions Jesus answered not a word. In anger Herod ordered guards to torture Jesus until he answered him; but still he answered not a word. Then Herod sent a message to Pilate saying: "I yield to you my rights as judge, because you are superior to me in power. I will approve of any judgment you may render in this case."

Again Jesus was brought to Pilate's court.

Pilate could not find the Nazarene guilty of a crime. He went into an inner room, and sat in silent thought. His wife came to him, and said: "Pilate, beware of what you do this hour." She told him of a vision she had seen the night before of Jesus, as he walked upon the waters and calmed an angry storm and of Jerusalem in blood; and the earth shaken like a reed before the wind. She said: "I pray you, Pilate, hearken unto me: Touch not this man from Galilee; he is a holy man." She left him, and Pilate wept.

When Pilate was assured that civil war would follow if he did not heed the wishes of the mob, he took a bowl of water, and in the presence of the multitude he washed his hands, and said: "This man whom you accuse, is son of the most holy God, and I proclaim my innocence. If you would shed his blood, his blood is on your hands, and not on mine."

The Jews exclaimed: "Let his blood be on our hands and on our children's hands." They led him forth toward the hill beyond the city's gates; they stoned him; spit upon him; and smote him with their hands. As he lay all bruised upon the ground, a Pharisee called out that Herod's guards were coming, and they would crucify him.

Beside the city gate they found Barabbas' cross. They lifted Jesus from the ground, and drove him on. He could not bear his cross; and Simon, a friend of Jesus, bore it on to Calvary.

Judas was with the mob. He thought Jesus would assert his power, and free himself; and when he saw his master bleeding upon the ground he said: "O God, what have I done?" He ran in haste to the temple door, and threw the silver upon the floor, and said to the priests: "Take back your bribe; it is the cost price of my soul; I have betrayed the son of God." He went away bowed in grief, and hung himself beyond the city's walls, and died.

Close beside Jesus were the Mary's, Miriam, and other women. When Jesus saw them weeping, he said: "Weep not for me, for though I go away, go through the gateway of the cross, yet on the next day of the sun, lift up your hearts, for I will meet you at the sepulcher."

Four Roman soldiers of Herod's guard were called to execute the orders of the court. They had tortured Jesus, had put a crown of thorns upon his head, had wrapped him in a royal robe, and mocked him. They stripped him, laid him on the cross, and took the nails the Jews had brought, and drove them through his hands and feet. They raised the cross between the crosses of two criminals.

Pilate had prepared a tablet. It was placed upon the cross; on it was written in Hebrew, Latin, and Greek these words of truth: "JESUS THE CHRIST. KING OF THE JEWS."

The Jews were angered at the words, but Pilate said: "What I have written, I have written; let it stand."

The soldiers and the mob sat down to watch Jesus die.

Jesus prayed: "My Father-God, forgive these men; they know not what they do."

One of the criminals joined others of the mob in mocking Jesus; the other said to Him: "When thou comest on the clouds of heaven, remember me." Jesus said: "Behold, I will meet you in the realm of souls this day."

Standing near the cross were many women, among them Mary, mother of the Lord, Miriam, Mary Magdalene, Martha, Ruth, and Mary, and Salome. And John stood near.

Jesus said to John: "In your most tender care I leave my mother and my sister Miriam."

At the sixth hour of the day it became as dark as night.
Men sought lanterns, and built fires upon the hills that
they might see.

Jesus exclaimed: "Heloi! Heloi! lama sabachthani?
(Thou sun! Thou sun! why hast thou forsaken me?")

At the ninth hour of the day the earth began to tremble;
a flood of golden light appeared above the cross, and from
the light a voice was heard which said: "Lo, it is done."
Jesus said: "My Father-God, into thy hands I give my
soul."

A Roman soldier in compassion pierced Jesus' heart,
and the son of man was dead.

The city of Jerusalem rocked to and fro, the hills were
rent, and tombs were opened up. The temple quivered,
and the veil between the sanctuary and the Holy Place
was rent in twain. A Roman guard exclaimed: "This
surely was the son of God who died."

The Scribes, the Priests, and Pharisees were filled with
fear; they hurried down from Calvary, and sought their
synagogues and homes.

Two aged Jews, Rabbi Joseph, the Arimathean counsel-
lor, and Nicodemus went to Pilate, and prayed that they
might take the body of Jesus and lay it in a tomb. Pilate
gave consent. They took the body of the Lord; and when
they had prepared it with spices, they laid it in a new-
made tomb that had been made for Joseph in a solid rock.
They rolled a stone up to the sepulcher.

The priests requested Pilate to send a guard to guard
the body of the Nazarine that friends might not take it,
and say that he had risen from the dead. Pilate said:
"You may send a hundred Jewish soldiers with a centurion
to guard the tomb."

The tomb was in the garden of Siloam near Joseph's
home. Caiaphas sent priests to see that Jesus' body was
in the tomb, and Pilate sent a Scribe to place the seal of
Rome upon the stone before the sepulcher. Then the soldier's watch began.

THE RESURRECTION AND ASCENSION OF JESUS

PART TWO

At midnight the tomb became a blaze of light. A troup of white-clad soldiers marched and countermarched before the door. The Jewish soldiers charged but not a white-clad soldier fell. They were the Silent Brotherhood. They marched among the frightened men. In fear the Jewish soldiers fled, and fell upon the ground.

The light grew dim; the white-clad soldiers marched away, and when the guards returned they saw that the stone and Roman seal were not disturbed.

While Jesus' body lay in the tomb, the Atman self of Jesus went forth and taught in the realm of soul. He opened prison doors, and freed the captives. He met the Masters of olden times, and told the story of his life on earth, and of his death in sacrifice for man, and of his promise to arise and walk with his disciples again in the garb of flesh, to prove to them the possibilities of man: that they might have the key to life and death and the resurrection of the dead.

The Masters sat in council and talked about the revelations of the coming age, when the Holy Breath would fill the earth and air, and would open up to man the way to perfection and endless life.

All was silent in the garden of Siloam on the Sabbath day. At midnight a voice was heard which said: Adon Mashich, Cumi; which meant, Lord Christ, arise. It seemed as though the voice was everywhere. The soldiers saw no man; and, though they blanched with fear, they stood and watched.

Just before the sun arose the heavens blazed with light, the earth began to tremble and a form descended. They heard again: "Adon Mashich, Cumi." The white-robed form tramped upon the Roman seal and tore it into shreds; he cast the great stone aside.

Jesus opened up his eyes, and said: "All hail the rising

sun! the coming of the day of righteousness! He folded his burial gown, his head bands, and coverings, and laid them all aside.

The stronger soldiers saw him rise, and stand beside the white-robed form; they saw his body change from mortal to immortal form, and then it disappeared, and then they heard a voice that sounded everywhere; it said: "Peace, Peace on earth; good will to men." The Lord had risen as he had said he would.

The soldiers hurried to Jerusalem to tell the priests that Jesus had risen from the dead.

Caiaphas called a council of the Jews; and, that the news should not go forth that Jesus had risen from the dead, they paid each soldier to say, that, while they slept, friends of the Nazarine came and stole the body from the tomb.

(Jesus permitted his body to die upon the cross to prove that death of the body does not touch the eternal Atman Self; that death is part of the carnal dream, the last enemy, that must be overcome.)

In John 11:25, 26, we read, Jesus said: "I am the resurrection, and the life: he that believeth in me, though he were dead yet shall he live; and whosoever liveth and believeth in me shall never die. Believeth thou this?"

In overcoming death, the last enemy, Jesus fulfilled his mission to the children of earth, "Knowing that Christ being raised from the dead dieth no more; death hath no more dominion over him." (Rom. 6:9.)

(Though man lives in the carnal self, yet shall he live in Christ. Each initiate who walks upon the Christ path that leads to conscious immortality, will suffer the carnal self to die through renunciation and purification. He shall pass from generation into regeneration; and, when human regeneration is complete, resurrection will follow. The carnal self is crucified upon the cross, and laid within the tomb before Atman, the Divine Self, is freed from the bondage of personality. And even as Jesus was assisted

from power on high to arise from the tomb in his resurrected body, so all that follow in his footsteps will be
assisted into the resurrected Christ.)

On the first day of the week, Mary, the mother of Jesus,
Miriam, and Mary Magdalene hastened to the tomb with
spices to embalm the Lord; and when they found the
empty tomb they grieved. Mary Magdalene ran toward
Jerusalem; and, at the gate, she met Peter, James, and
John. She told them that someone had carried off the body
of the Lord; and they returned to the tomb in haste.

Two Masters sat within the tomb. As Mary looked
within they said: "Why do you weep?" Mary said: "Because my Lord is gone; someone has carried off the body of
my Lord; I know not where it is."

A man stood near. Mary thought it was the gardener.
He came near, and said: "My Mother!" and Mary said:
"My Lord." Miriam's eyes were opened up and she beheld the Lord, and Jesus said: "Behold, I told you as we
walked along the way up to the cross that I would meet
you at the sepulcher upon the first day of the week."

Jesus went to Mary Magdalene and said: "Why seek
the living among the dead? Your Lord has risen as he
said. Now, Mary, look! behold my face."

Mary Magdalene was filled with joy, and sought again
for Peter, James, and John; and said to them: "Lo, I have
seen the Lord, and Mary, and Miriam, and many others
have seen him; for he has risen from the dead."

The disciples did not believe; they thought it was a
vision. Then John beheld a stranger coming up the walk.
The stranger raised his hands and spoke a word; and then
they knew it was the Lord. He said to them: Behold, for
human flesh can be transmuted into higher form, and then
that higher form is master of things manifest, and can, at
will, take any form.

And Jesus told them to go to Thomas and the other
men and say, that, he whom Jews and Romans thought
was dead, was walking in the garden of Siloam; and that

he would stand again before the Priests and Pharisees in the temple in Jerusalem; and would appear unto the sages of the world; and that he would go before them into Galilee.

Zachus and Cleophas were friends of Jesus; and, toward evening of the resurrection day, as they were going to their home at Emmaus, a stranger joined them. While they walked, they talked of Jesus, and of the things that had transpired, and of his resurrection from the dead.

The stranger told them many things about the Christ, and when they reached their home they ate the evening meal together. The stranger took bread, and blessed it in the name of Christ; and they perceived he was the Lord. Then Jesus disappeared. The two returned, at once, to Jerusalem; and everywhere they said: "Lo, we have seen the Lord."

Jesus appeared to ten disciples in Simon's home in Bethany. At first they thought he was a phantom; but when they felt his form and saw him eat they knew that it was the resurrected Lord.

At his home, Lazarus was talking with Mary, Ruth, and Martha about the rumor of the risen Lord. Jesus appeared in their midst, and said: "All Hail! for I am risen from the dead, first fruitage of the grave!" And then they talked a long time about the trial, and Calvary, and the garden of Siloam; and Jesus said: "Fear not, for I will be your boon companion all the way." Then he disappeared.

At the palace of Prince Ravanna in India, Jesus appeared during a feast, given in honor of the wise men of the east. He entered unannounced, and raised his hands in benediction, and said: "All Hail!" He sat down in a vacant chair at the table to the east. A halo rested on his head, and light filled all the room. Then the wise men knew it was the Hebrew prophet who had come.

Jesus said: "Behold, for I am risen from the dead. Look at my hands, my feet, my side. The Roman soldiers pierced my hands and feet with nails; and then one pierced my heart. They put me in a tomb, and then I wrestled with the conqueror of men. I conquered death, I stamped upon him, and arose; brought immortality to light, and painted on the walls of time a rainbow for the sons of men; and what I did all men shall do."

And all India heard these words of life.

Then Jesus appeared to the Magian priests in Persepolis. Among them were the three who were first to greet him as babe in Bethlehem. Jesus said to them: "My brothers of the Silent Brotherhood, peace, peace on earth; good will to men! The problem of the ages has been solved; a son of man has risen from the dead; has shown that human flesh can be transmuted into flesh divine." He told the story of his mission to the sons of men, and then he disappeared.

Then Jesus appeared in the temple in Jerusalem in the garb of a fisherman. He questioned the Scribes and Pharisees concerning Jesus, who was called the Christ. They told him that he was crucified and that his body had been stolen from the tomb. The fisherman became a radiant form of light. The Scribes and Pharisees fell back in deadly fear. They saw the man from Galilee. Looking upon them, Jesus said: "This is the body that you stoned beyond the city's gates, and crucified on Calvary. Behold my hands, my feet, my side; and see the wounds the soldiers made. If you believe that I am phantom of the air, come forth, and handle me; ghosts do not carry flesh and bones. I came to earth to demonstrate the resurrection of the dead, the transmutation of the flesh of carnal man to flesh of man divine." Then Jesus raised his hands, and said: "Peace be to everyone of you; good will to all mankind." Then he disappeared.

And Jesus stood before Apollo and the Silent Brotherhood of Greece as they were sitting in a Delphian grove. He said to them: "Behold, for I have risen from the dead with gifts for men. I bring to you the title of your vast estate. All power in heaven and earth is mine; to you I give all power in heaven and earth. Go forth, and teach

the nations of the earth the gospel of the resurrection of
the dead and of eternal life through Christ, the love of
God made manifest to men." He clasped Apollo's hand,
and said: "My human flesh was changed to higher form
by love divine, and I can manifest in flesh, or in the higher
planes of life, at will. What I can do all men can do. Go,
preach the gospel of the omnipotence of man."

He then appeared to Claudas and Juliet in Rome. These
servants of Tiberius were on the Tiber in a boat. A storm
swept in from the sea and they were sinking down to
death. Jesus took them by the hands, and said: "Claudas
and Juliet, arise, and walk with me upon the waves." A
thousand people saw them reach the land. Jesus said to
them: "You men of Rome, I am the resurrection and the
life. They that are dead shall live, and many that shall
live will never die. Claudas and Juliet are my ambassadors to Rome. They will point the way and preach the
gospel of the Holy Breath and of the resurrection of the
dead."

The priests of Heliopolis knew that Jesus had risen from
the dead. He appeared before them and stood upon a
sacred pedestal which had been reserved for him who first
would demonstrate the resurrection of the dead. The Masters stood, and said: "All Hail!" The temple blazed with
light and the temple bells rang out. Jesus said: "All
honor to the Masters of the Temple of the Sun."

And he told them that in the flesh of man was the essence of the resurrection of the dead; and, when quickened
by the Holy Breath, this essence raised the substance of the
body to a higher tone. That, in death, the essence of the
body was breathed upon by God just as God breathed
upon the chaos of the deep when worlds were formed; and
that life springs forth from death, and the carnal form is
changed to form divine. That the will of man makes pos-
sible the action of the Holy Breath; that when will of man
and will of God are one, the resurrection is a fact.

He told them that his life was one great drama for the
sons of men; that he was a pattern for them; and that he

lived to show the possibilities of man. He disappeared, and at the sea of Galilee appeared to his disciples. He talked, and ate the morning meal with them.

As the news spread forth that Jesus had risen from the dead, multitudes came, and saw the Lord.

He told Peter, James, and John that he would meet his apostles in Jerusalem. While there in prayer together, Jesus appeared, and gave them instructions to go forth, and preach the gospel of the Christ; the unity of God and man; the resurrection of the dead; and of eternal life. He said: "You know the sacred Word, which is the word of power. The secret things that I have told to you, that may not now be told to all the world, you shall make known to faithful men who shall in turn reveal them unto other faithful men, until the time shall come when all the world may hear and comprehend the words of truth and power. And now I will ascend to God as you and all the world will rise to God. Behold, upon the day of Pentecost you all shall be endowed with power from on high."

Then Jesus went to Olivet. His disciples followed. Near Bethany Jesus met the Mary's, Salome, Martha, Ruth, Miriam and Lazarus, and many others from Galilee. He stood apart and raised his hands and said: "The bene-dictions of the Holy Ones, of Almighty God, and of the Holy Breath, of Christ the love of God made manifest will rest upon you all the way till you shall rise and sit with me upon the throne of power."

They saw him rise upon the wings of light, encircled in a wreath, and then they saw his form no more.

Two men in robes of white appeared, and said: "Lo, he will come again from heaven as you have seen him go to heaven." (Aquarian Gospel, 161:180 in part.)

(Jesus ascended unto the Father in the vibration of Aum. He said to his disciples: "As I ascend to God so you and all the world will ascend to God." The ascension unto the Father reunites Atman with his Source, and He abides again at home, beyond that mystical wall which separates the world of relativity from Paradise, the Kingdom—Aum.)

LESSON XII.

THE ESTABLISHMENT OF THE CHRISTINE CHURCH
AND
THE MESSAGE OF THE NEW AGE

THROUGHOUT the Aquarian Gospel of Jesus, the Christ, we read of the life of Jesus, who came to manifest the love of God to men. The final chapter tells of the establishment of the Christine Church, after the great Master had finished His work amidst humanity in the outer world and had ascended unto God.

The events of the day of Pentecost, the endowment of the apostles with power from on high, and Peter's introductory sermon are given.

Three thousand people were baptized on that eventful day when Peter said: "The Christine Church is opened up, and whosoever will may enter in, and, by the boundless grace of Christ, be saved." And they became members of the Christine Church, that stands upon the postulates that Jesus is the love of God made manifest, and that love is savior of the sons of men. And on that day the Christine Church became a mighty power and Christ became a mighty word. (Aquarian Gospel, 181:182 in part.)

The Piscean age has closed, and the dawn of the New Day is at hand for the humanity of this planet. In this day, the dawn of the Aquarian age, the Universal Church is being established by Aum Jehovah, the Solar Deity, Jesus Christ, the Messiah, and their Ambassadors, the Masters in the Great White Brotherhood.

The message of the New Age comes forth through revelation from the Divine Source. It is the message of Aum,

113

the Absolute, which deals with God and His Spiritual Creation; the understanding and realization of which brings man into conscious sonship with Aum, the Father-Mother God.

In conscious sonship, Atman, the Divine self, the image and likeness of God, expresses.

This is realized through the path of Love and Wisdom, given in the Secret Heart Teaching, the esoteric message of Jesus Christ, which leads to redemption of the body, by following in the footsteps of those that have gone before, the Great Ones, who have reached the goal of at-one-ment with God. In love, wisdom and compassion the Masters of the White Brotherhood, Jesus Christ, the head, assist their younger brothers to climb the mountain of Truth, that they too, may reach the Kingdom—Aum.

Jesus said, nearly two thousand years ago: "I am the Way, the Truth, and the Life. No man cometh unto the Father except through me." Only through the door of the Christ can man reach the Father's house—Aum. Jesus taught this message, and proved the Truth unto full redemption of His body. He became the first fruit of the humanity of this planet and his instruction is: "Follow Me."

On Mount Olive, He ascended unto the Father in His glorified transmuted body, and He said to those who witnessed his ascension: "As I ascend to God, so you and all the world will ascend to God."

Jesus taught that man must be born again. This is a vital lesson in the message of the New Age. When man is sufficiently renounced to receive this gift from God, a ray of the Divine Spirit, Aum, comes to abide in form, in him. And It leads him into all Truth.

When man has reached the place upon the path in his search for Truth, where he is willing to don the robe of humility, and, in childlike simplicity desires only to know God, he is assisted to find his way out from the illusion of the world (the creation of the carnal mind of man) into the reality. Upon this pilgrimage of the soul every vestige of carnality must be overcome. As man casts aside the garments of the carnal man, he comes ever closer into the light of Truth.

The life and works of Jesus of Nazareth culminated in the outer, nearly two thousand years ago, by the help of Jehovah and the Elohim, in the resurrection of His body. He arose triumphantly from the tomb, and He ascended to heaven in the vibration of Aum. To-day He vibrates as the God-man.

It is the destiny of all humanity to reach heaven, the new Jerusalem, Aum. In the Revelation of St. John the Divine, we read: "And I saw a new heaven and a new earth: for the first heaven and the first earth were passed away; and there was no more sea." (Rev. 21:1.)

And I John saw the holy city, new Jerusalem, coming down from God out of heaven, prepared as a bride adorned for her husband. (Rev. 21:2.)

And he said unto me: "It is done. I am Alpha and Omega, the beginning and the end. I will give unto him that is athirst of the fountain of the water of life freely." (Rev. 21:6.)

He that overcometh shall inherit all things; and I will be his God, and he shall be my son. (Rev. 21:7.)

And the Spirit and the bride say, Come. And let him that heareth say come. And let him that is athirst come.

And whosoever will, let him take the water of life freely. (Rev. 22:17.)

The grace of our Lord Jesus Christ be with you all. Amen. (Rev. 22:21.)

Aum is Peace; Aum is Eternity. Aum is the Living Essence, the One God and man is of That and man is in That.

Aum Tat Sat Aum.

CONCLUSION

AUM, the Absolute, is Eternity. In Aum, time does not exist. In relativity, the natural world, ages come and go. The Piscean age has finished, and the dawn of the Aquarian Age is here.

The Kingdom of Peace will be established upon the earth in this New Day and the fruition of the message of Christianity will be given to humanity.

Immortality, in the body is the fulfillment of the message of Jesus Christ. This is Redemption. Jesus Christ proved the message when he brought immortality to light. He is the pattern for all humanity, and He said: "Follow Me."

Humanity is being quickened and attuned to hear the call of the Messiah, to comprehend the light of Aum, the living God, the Omnipresence, the Foundation and Essence of all manifestations; and this is the rock upon which the message of the New Age stands. It is the day of Scientific Knowing and, too, the day of Devotion. Every head will bow in reverence to the Supreme Spirit, Aum, and to Aum—Jehovah, the Personal God, the Deity of our solar system, whose throne rests in the supernal light of Aum, and to Jesus Christ, the Messiah.

In the silence of the Infinite Heart, Atman abides. To become conscious of this is at-one-ment with Aum, the great Father-Mother who fills all space, and enfolds within Itself Its divine creation and sustains all in love, through Its eternal action, the inbreathing and outbreathing of Holy Breath. Aum is Atman's abiding place, his home.

"The outer man comprehends not this abiding place. Not until the outer self is merged within the inner self will divinity, the perfect man, express consciously in Aum. This is Enlightenment. Jesus is the fully enlightened one, yea, so fully enlightened is He, that Jesus is merged into the Christ. His personality was absorbed in that great day when He ascended above; but His individuality stands, the resplendent glory of God, and moves in the heaven of heavens; and His Light, Love, and Glory is so great, and it extends to earth in such power, that all who call unto the Father in His name are blessed according to their righteous desires." (Flashlights of Truth.)

The Great Master was assisted by the Father and the Elohim into the glory Presence, Aum, and each of God's children will be assisted likewise, when they reach the period of fruition.

The perfect man will abide in the glory of God's presence, filling his place in action, a redeemed Son of God.

"When the millennium is established upon earth, of which we are now in the dawn, the Sons of God who have become conscious, will live in the midst of a perfect civilization; and Christ will reign supreme, and Jesus Christ will be the King, because He, the conscious Elder Son, is heir to the outer throne. But each man, also, is a king, and a priest unto God; and his heart is God's throne, and He dwells there forevermore.

The Glory of God, Aum, will be so great in that bright day, that none but the enlightened ones can abide upon earth; for, lo, it is become heaven, and none but the pure in heart and illumined in mind and regenerated in body will be able to dwell there." (Flashlights of Truth.)

Then all upon the earth may sing in one accord: "Lo, I have seen the Light, Mine eyes hath seen the Glory of the Lord."

Supreme Spirit, Father—Aum!
Draw all Thy wand'ring children home,
And in Thy loving soft embrace
Hold them securely, 'till by Thy Grace
They see Thee, Father, face to face.

Supreme Spirit, Mother Divine,
Holy Breath—Love Essence Sublime
In Love's pure action, that ne'er will cease,
Sing tenderly to Atman,
Thy lullaby, of Light and Life and Joy and Peace.